LEATHERWORK

A PRACTICAL GUIDE

The author in his workshop.

LEATHERWORK
A PRACTICAL GUIDE

CHRIS TAYLOR

THE CROWOOD PRESS

First published in 2009 by
The Crowood Press Ltd
Ramsbury, Marlborough
Wiltshire SN8 2HR

www.crowood.com

British Library Cataloguing-in-Publication Data
A catalogue record for this book is available from the British Library.

ISBN 978 1 84797 136 4

Photographs by Chris Taylor and Ian Wilson.
Line drawings by Chris Taylor.

Acknowledgements
Abbey Saddlery & Crafts Ltd for allowing us to photograph in their warehouse. J & E Sedgwicks & Co Ltd, Walsall (curriers of leather for the equestrian trade) for their time and information.

Please Note
As the majority of people are right-handed, including myself, the techniques described are from a right-handed person's perspective. It would be tedious to describe every technique in both left- and right-handed manners. If this upsets anyone, I apologize; but I must emphasize that it is easy to adapt and all the left-handed students that I have taught have never had a problem.

Disclaimer
Safety is of the utmost importance in every aspect of leatherwork. When using tools and chemicals, always follow the manufacturer's recommended procedures. The author and publisher cannot accept responsibility for any accident or injury caused by following the advice given in this book.

Typeset by Sara Millington
Printed and bound in Malaysia by Times Offset (M) Sdn Bhd

CONTENTS

Dedication

To my family, who have been a constant source of encouragement.
I would also like to give a special mention to my niece, Alex – the best person I have ever met.

INTRODUCTION

Welcome to the wonderful world of leather, a beautiful material with exceptional versatility. Up until the development of synthetic materials, leather could be found in many industries and walks of life. Apart from its use in equestrian equipment, leather was used in bellows, washers, fire hoses, buckets, drinking vessels (known as 'Jacks'), as well as in clothing and shoes.

Although the first use of leather is unknown, it is not unreasonable to assume that early man would have quickly realized the potential of animal skins as a source of warmth and protection from the elements. Archaeological evidence has given us an insight into how old and how important the craft of leather working was. Although techniques in preserving the animal skins (tanning) may have changed the skills and tools developed to work the leather have changed little over the centuries. Today it is still a fascinating and rewarding craft which lends itself to self-expression.

This book has been written to encourage the absolute beginner and to impart advanced skills to the more experienced leatherworker, with detailed descriptions and instructions on the use of tools and techniques. The projects range from the very simple basic projects to the more advanced such as horse bridles.

As a working Master Saddler, I use some terms and names of tools that may differ from those in general leatherwork. Where possible the generic terms have also been given.

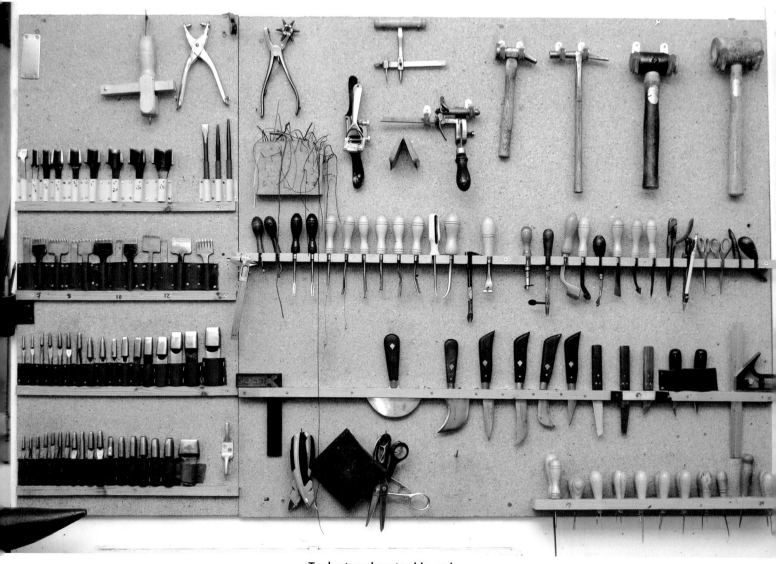

Tools stored on tool board.

CHAPTER 1

TOOLS

People say they always know if a stranger has been driving their car. The same can be said of tools, as they become very personalized. I always know if someone has used my round knife, and touch my stitching awls at your peril! My apprentices have their own set of tools, while students on training courses are allocated a set.

Browse through any leatherworking catalogue and you will see a vast array of strange and confusing tools. Obviously you do not need all of them, and what you purchase will depend on your circumstances. Good quality tools are always an asset and should last much longer than cheaper equivalents, but if they are only for occasional use then a lesser quality tool may be adequate.

The best advice is for you to decide what your first project is going to be and buy the tools necessary to do the job. Then add to them as you see fit. Quite often tools intended for other crafts can be adapted for use with leatherwork. (A woodworker's spoke shave, for example, can be used as a skiver, providing the blade is honed and polished.) It would be impracticable to describe every tool on the market so I hope that by describing a selection of tools that I consider the most useful you can make an informed decision as to which items to purchase.

Guidelines on workshop safety are discussed at the end of this chapter. You will be using sharp tools that can cause serious injury so it is worth setting yourself a workshop safety standard from the outset.

Stitching Requisites

Various items required for stitching: stitching and loop clams, threads, needles and beeswax.

Awls

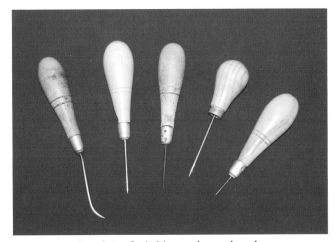

A variety of stitching and scratch awls.

STITCHING AWL

This is possibly the most personalized tool in the workshop. The handles and blades, which come in varying sizes and shapes, are purchased separately and have to be made up. A pear shaped handle and 2in (50mm) straight blade will suffice for all but the heaviest of leathers. Awl blades are quite brittle and will snap with misuse so always have spare handles and blades to hand.

Assembling the Awl

The blade will have an end with a black tempered finish that goes into the handle, and a shiny end. To assemble the awl place the blade vertically in a vice with the tempered end showing, ensuring that the jaws of the vice are covered with a soft material to avoid damaging the blade surface. There will be a hole drilled in the tapered end of the handle, place this over the blade and using a mallet tap it into position leaving 1–1¼in (25–30mm) protruding. Make sure that the handle is in line with the blade.

Close inspection of the blade will reveal a diamond shape with a rough surface and sharp point. If used in this condition the blade will snag the leather fibres making penetration difficult, so we need to polish the blade to allow it to cut cleanly through the leather. For this you will need a pair of electrical side cutters, fine wet and dry emery paper, a small block of wood, a piece of scrap leather and water. First wrap the emery paper around the block of wood and sprinkle water onto it (the water acts as a lubricant). Using the side cutters snip off the awl point. Then work the blade against the emery paper until it is smooth and polished (if the emery paper dries out, sprinkle more water onto it). This method of using fine wet and dry emery paper can be used to finely hone knife blades, but watch your fingers and always wrap the emery paper around a wooden block.

We use the wooden block to maintain the blade's original diamond shape; the long sides should be as knife edges, not rounded, while the tip needs to be rounded with the end again being sharpened to a knife edge.

Periodically try to push the awl through the scrap leather. As the blade becomes polished you will notice the ease in which it slides through the leather. The awl is ready for use when it passes cleanly through the leather without snagging the fibres. Getting the awl to run smoothly is tedious and can take a long time, but persevere as you will reap the rewards for your efforts when you start stitching.

Placing the awl blade into the handle absolutely square is very difficult. For this reason make a notch in the handle in line with one of the flat faces of the blade. It should be large enough to be felt easily with your thumb. While stitching, if your thumb is always in this notch the blade will run through the leather at the same angle. If the blade keeps slipping out of the handle, or the hole in the end of the handle is too big, put a drop of super glue into the hole before tapping the handle into place and leave it for a few minutes to set.

If the blade breaks it nearly always breaks flush with the handle. There is a theory that the handle can be drilled and reused or a new blade can be tapped in alongside the broken end. Personally I just get a new handle and blade and start afresh. I have tried the two methods mentioned and found that they involve a lot of fiddling without much success. The best method is not to break the awl.

SCRATCH AWL

On heavier leathers, when marking out patterns or straight lines it is better to use a deep scratch line rather than drawing on it with a pen. Knife blades tend to follow a scratch line more easily than a pen or pencil mark. Having put a lot of effort into preparing your stitching awl the last thing you want to do is to ruin the end by using it for marking out leather. Instead we use a scratch awl. Any object with a point on the end will do, although clicker's awls are cheap, come complete with handle and blade and make ideal scratch awls.

ROUND AWL

Like stitching awls, round awls come in two parts, a handle and blade. They are made up in the same manner as the stitching awl but do not have to be polished. As they do not have a sharpened blade they are useful when stitching over existing stitching because they do not cut the stitches. They can also be used as scratch awls.

Stitching Clams (Saddler's Clams)

There are various sorts of stitching clams in use, but they all perform the same function – to hold your work in place leaving your hands free. Whichever ones you use is down to personal choice.

Saddler's clams are made from two pieces of specially shaped wood that are bolted together at the base. The pieces are shaped so that a sprung set of jaws are formed on the top. A bolt and wing nut placed further up the clams allows the

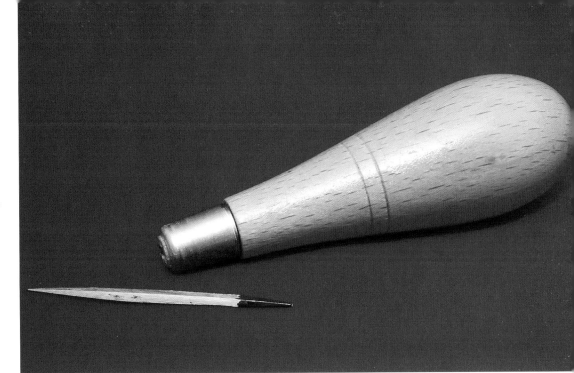

Awls are purchased in two parts: handle and blade.

ASSEMBLING THE AWL

Place the blade into a vice; to protect the blade cover the jaws with a soft material.

Tap the handle into place.

The right and wrong way to finish the points on a new awl blade.

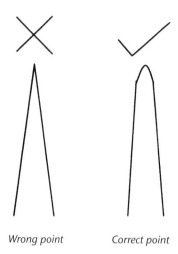

Wrong point   *Correct point*

tension on the jaws to be adjusted. On the inside of the clams is a staple. This is to accommodate a strap, called a stirrup, which is used to steady the clams and increase the pressure on the jaws if required. It also makes a handy foot rest. This type of clam is designed to be held between the knees, and as they are quite long you will need a high chair; a draughtsman chair is ideal.

A stitching pony consists of a bench with the clams fixed to one end. The position of the clam is set and cannot be adjusted. Some models have sprung jaws, the tension being adjusted by a wing nut at the base of the clams, while others require pressure to be exerted on some form of foot lever to close the jaws. To use the stitching pony, you sit astride the bench with the clams in front of you.

SETTING UP CLAMS
Whichever clams you choose the jaws should be covered with leather to protect the work. Cut two pieces of soft leather the same width as the jaws and approximately 6in (152mm) long. Remove the tensioning bolt and the two pieces should slide apart. Tack the leather over the jaws, replace the tensioning bolt and tighten to desired tension.

This may differ on stitching ponies in which case you will need to examine them carefully and decided how best to part

them. If you are using a stitching pony then no further setup is required.

On saddler's clams, the next step is to place the stirrup. Opposite the staple will be a slot – run the strap through this slot, around the staple and back through the slot. With the clams between your knees and resting against your left thigh, adjust the strap so that your foot rests comfortably within the loop. As you get more practised at using the clams you will probably find that the stirrup will need re-adjusting to obtain the optimum level.

The stirrup does not need to be made of leather – a strong piece of string tied in a knot at the right length will suffice, and while it is not essential it will prove very useful. Not all clams will have the staple and slot to accommodate the stirrup. The staples can be purchased, and it is a fairly simple task to place it and cut a slot opposite for the stirrup strap.

Loop clams
These can be thought of as miniature clams that fit into the jaws of the stitching clams. Their purpose is to hold keepers (loops) in place while being stitched. They are certainly a useful item if doing a lot of strapwork but not essential.

Stitch Markers (Pricking Irons)

These are sometimes known as pricking irons and are used to mark the leather ready for stitching. They come in a variety of stitch lengths ranging from 3–12 stitches per inch (25mm). They also come in a variety of widths, the most common being ½in (12mm), 1in (25mm) and 1½in (37mm). When starting out a good general purpose stitch marker is a 1 inch (25mm) marker with a stitch length of 8 per inch (25mm).

The stitch marker is not used to punch through the leather, merely to mark the surface. Place the stitch marker on the leather at the required position. Holding it firmly and at 90 degrees to the leather, give the end a sharp tap with a mallet. The marks need to be heavy enough to be seen when stitching.

Pricking Wheel

Another form of stitch marker is the pricking wheel. These come either as a complete unit or as a frame with interchangeable pricking wheels, which are rolled across the surface of the leather. These tools leave an adequate impression on natural vegetable tanned leathers, but on leather with dyed waxed surfaces the marks are difficult to see, and while they are quicker than stitch markers care must be exercised when using these as they can easily veer off line.

Needles

Contrary to popular belief the most commonly used needles for hand stitching are blunt to help reduce the possibility of splitting the threads. They are known as saddler's harness needles and range in sizes from 1 to 4, with 1 being the largest and 4 the smallest. Further sizes 1/0, 2/0 and 3/0 are available for heavier threads (1/0 being the smallest, which is the reverse of the standard needle sizes).

If you intend to do any lacing (thonging) you will require a lacing needle. These differ from conventional needles in that they are flat and do not have an eye. Instead they have a flat sprung end that opens to accommodate the lace. One surface has two prongs that pierce the lace holding it secure.

Threads

The main threads used for hand stitching are made from linen and come in various thicknesses and colours. The thickness of the thread (commonly referred to as thread weight) is denoted by the thickness of a single strand followed by the number of strands twisted together to make up the thread. The most commonly used threads from the thinnest to thickest are 18/3, 18/4, 18/5 and 18/6. There are also finer threads such as 25/3 and heavier threads such as 16/3; the list of thread weights available would probably fill this book.

EXPLANATION OF THREAD WEIGHTS

Thread making is a centuries-old tradition and consequently gives us wonderful terms such as hanks and skeins, which have been mostly lost in our modern world. So long as you remember that 25/3 threads are thinner than 18/3s, which in turn are thinner than 18/6s, that is all that is required, but this section will hopefully give an insight into how these designations are acquired and will provide you to with an entry to the mystical world of thread making.

The strand thickness is calculated by weight against length, from a static weight of 1lb (approx 450g). Cotton threads are calculated in hanks while linen thread uses skeins (1 hank = 18yd or approx 16m; 1 skein = 300yd or approx 277m). To make a linen thread marked as '18', the fibres from 1lb (450g) weight of linen would be stretched out in a continuous length to make 18 skeins. This would give a strand length of 5,400yd (approx 4985m); 18 skeins × 300yd (277m). Subsequently, to make a thread marked '25' the fibres would be stretched out to make 25 skeins giving a continuous length of 7,500yd (approx 6923m); 25 skeins × 300yd (277m).

This gives the first part of the notation marked on threads. The second part refers to the number of strands that are twisted together. Hence 18/3 thread would have three strands of linen that have been stretched out to 5,400yd (4985m) twisted together; and although a 25/3 thread also has three strands, each strand has been stretched to 7,500yd (6923m), thus making it thinner than a 18/3 thread.

HANDMADE THREADS

The majority of threads purchased will be ready made, but balls consisting of a continuous fine linen strand can be

The materials used for hand making threads.

obtained for the purpose of making your own thread. While this is generally the domain of saddlers working on heavy horse harness where thicker threads are required, it can be used to great effect on general leatherworking projects especially where a rough rustic effect is required.

The strand is pulled from the centre of the ball, which can collapse and tangle very easily. To prevent this it is a good idea to make a box to keep the ball in. When making a thread you will need something to hook the strands over, and if you intend to make a lot of threads it is useful to make a thigh pad.

For this explanation I have used a cup hook screwed into the workbench and will be making a thread consisting of eight strands. Beeswax and a small piece of thin leather will be needed (a piece of cloth may be used if the leather is not available) and make sure that they are placed within reach.

1. Hold the end of the strand in the left hand and place it over the hook. Move closer or further from the hook to adjust the length of the thread, ensuring that the two resulting sides are equal.

2. To break the strand, use the palm of the hand to roll the strand in the right hand against the right thigh while exerting a slight pull.

3. Line up the ends of the strands in the left hand and repeat processes 1 and 2 until the required number of strands to make the thread have been achieved. From this point on I will refer to the strands in the right hand as Bundle A and the ones in the left hand as Bundle B. (Left handed people can start with the end of the strand in the right hand and breaking the strand on the left thigh if required).

4. Using the fingers to keep the two bundles separate, transfer Bundle A into the left hand, then liberally apply the beeswax to both bundles in turn.

5. Return Bundle A to the right hand and roll it against the right thigh, thus twisting the strands together to form the thread. Keep rolling until a tight twist is achieved, then switch Bundle B to the right hand and repeat the process.

6. Wax the twisted bundles. Then using the thin leather between the thumb and forefinger, grasp the thread and rapidly rub the thread to remove any excess wax and help to melt the wax into the thread.

7. If done correctly the ends of the thread will be tapered. Trim the thin ends but leave the taper as this allows a thinner needle to be used. The thread is now ready for use.

Beeswax

Linen threads used in their natural state would quickly be shredded with the constant pulling through the leather, so they need to be waxed before use. Threads can be purchased pre-waxed but it is cheaper to buy the wax and threads separately. Wax is normally purchased in 1oz (28.35g) blocks. Most people use it direct from the packet, which is perfectly acceptable, but mixing it with boiled linseed oil gives it a softer, stickier consistency. To do this melt the wax over a gentle heat source then add the linseed, the amount depends on how soft you like the wax but 2–3tbsp to 4oz (113g) of wax is a good starting point. Pour a small amount into a bucket of cold water, work it into a ball and leave it to dry for a couple of days when it will be ready for use.

Over a period of time the wax block will pick up bits of thread, fluff and dirt, making it necessary to change it. Do not throw away the old wax – just put it to one side and when you have accumulated enough of them melt them down as described above. Pouring the wax through a flour sieve will remove the dirt. Unless you enjoy plumbing and are prepared to spend hours trying to unblock pipes, do not be tempted to do this in the kitchen sink!

Sundries

Other items required for stitching are a small pair of pliers for pulling through stubborn needles and a small pair of sharp scissors for thread cutting.

Knives

Knives for cutting leather come in all shapes and sizes, and it can be confusing as to which is required. There are leather scissors (known as leather shears) available, but they are really only suited to the thinner leathers. A sharp knife will give a cleaner cut than scissors.

Round Knives

The round knife is a very versatile tool and although not essential, the purchase of one is highly recommended. In the Roman Army Museum at the Roman fort of Vindolanda, Hadrian's Wall, there is a round knife that was found in the cobbler's shop, and you could be excused for thinking that it had come from a modern day leatherwork shop. Metals may have changed, but the shape of the round knife has remained the same for centuries.

There are varying sizes of round knives and, although beginners may find the smaller sizes easier to handle, mastering any of the available sizes is not too difficult given practice. Purchasing cheap round knives is false economy. The metals are of poor quality, difficult to sharpen and lose their edge quickly.

There are half round knives (also called head knives) which are basically as the name would suggest, half a round knife and are used in the same manner. The difference in cost between the two is minimal, but some people find them easier to master.

INITIAL PREPARATION

The cutting edge on any new knife will have been sharpened on a grinding wheel at the factory, giving the blade a rough texture. Try the knife on a leather scrap and you will find that it cuts, but like a new stitching awl blade it snags the leather fibres. Hone the blade using the wet and dry emery paper in the same manner used when making up a new stitching awl, or strop it on your sharpening strop (the making of which will be covered later on in this chapter).

CUTTING

Mark a straight line on a scrap piece of leather using the scratch awl. It is important to keep the edge of the cut square, so hold the round knife at 90 degrees to the leather with the curve of the blade on the line. Following the line, push the knife away from you making sure that your fingers are to the side. The main mistake that beginners make is to put too much pressure on the knife in an attempt to cut through the leather in one go, resulting in the blade digging into the work surface or skidding off the surface. It is better to use a lighter pressure and go over the line two or three times; once the first cut is

Working clockwise from 12 o'clock: round knife, half round knife, general purpose knife, clicker's knife and Stanley knife.

Using the round knife to cut a straight line.

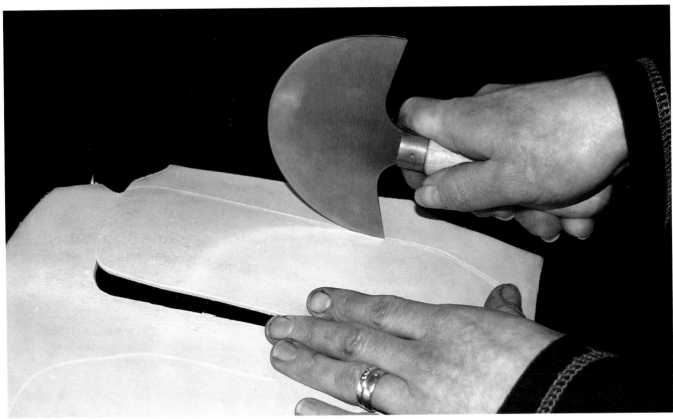

Cutting shapes with the round knife; the blade is tipped back for easier cutting of curves.

made you will find that the blade wants to follow the cut line on the second and/or third passes. If the blade starts to lose its edge while working, flip it over and use the other side.

Another method is to hold the round knife as described, place it on the edge of the line and roll it forward. Move along the line using a 'rocking' motion. Beginners often feel that they have more control using this method, but it is laborious and the finished cut is often ragged. Try to persevere with the first method.

Once you are confident with cutting straight lines mark a shape on the leather, initially avoiding sharp angles or curves. Holding the blade at 90 degrees to the leather and use the point of the knife to go around the outline. The same principles for cutting straight lines apply; do not put too much pressure on the knife and be patient. To negotiate curves, tilt the knife towards you so that the knife is cutting on its point.

SAFETY

Blunt knives cause accidents as the blade does not bite into the leather and skids off. Make sure the knife is sharp. In my own workshop I always make a point of stropping my knife before starting a job. Always be aware of the position of your fingers – this is especially relevant when cutting shapes where it is easy to get your hand in front of the knife. Pay attention to your workshop safety standard (*see* end of chapter).

Craft Knives

If you do not wish to purchase a round knife, then you will require some form of craft knife, Stanley knife or clicker's knife to cut your leather. If using a Stanley knife the carpet cutting blades are best. These blades are hook shaped which makes it easier to follow lines. Most of these types of knives have disposable blades. However, there is no need to be wasteful – these blades can be sharpened and re-used, and often they run better the more they are sharpened. A clicker's knife is a very useful implement to have around the workshop even if you have a round knife.

CUTTING AND SAFETY

While the round knife is pushed away from you, craft knives are drawn towards you but the same principles of cutting and safety with the round knife apply. When the blade is new it may snag the leather fibres; in this circumstance it will require honing as previously described.

General Purpose Knife

To maintain your knives in good order they should only be used for the purpose that they were intended, so a general purpose knife is useful for doing all the other tasks (such as cutting parcel strings) where a knife is required.

Cutting Mats

Strictly speaking this is more of an accessory than a tool. It not only prevents you getting grief from your partner after you have gouged a large groove out of the dining room table, but it also helps reduce the wear on the blades of knives as wood will blunt a knife very quickly. Even if you have a dedicated work bench, cutting directly onto the surface will soon produce grooves which the knife blades will want to follow when cutting through leather. There are different types of mat, but I find the self-healing type approximately 24 × 18in (610 × 460mm) suitable, and they are available at most craft or stationery stores. In my workshop they take a lot of hammer and are used every day, but they still last three to four years. They can be used for punching, but it is not recommended as this will reduce their lifespan and the smaller punches tend to go through them.

Punches

Hole Punch

Hole punches can be purchased as single punches or as punch pliers. Single punches range in size from approximately $1/16$in (1.5mm) to $5/8$in (16mm) in diameter. The method of identifying and the range of sizes available will vary between countries and manufacturers; some use a numbering system while others will give the diameter size. Where a numbering system is employed the range is normally 1–16, with 1 being the smallest.

Punch pliers consist of an anvil and punch attached to either of the jaws. On some the punch is static and is unscrewed to accommodate varying sizes while on others there is a revolving head which accommodates the first six sizes of punch, these are generally known as revolving punches. A good quality pair of punch pliers should meet all your initial requirements.

There are also oval-hole punches and as the name implies they punch oval holes. They can be used to great effect on wide belts and give easier passage for the tongues of heavier buckles. These punches are identified in the same manner as hole punches, but the numbering system can be more confusing (for example in the saddlery trade oval punches are numbered 17 to 25). It is worth noting that where an actual size value is given it relates to the length of the oval not the width.

Wad punches, so called because they were developed to cut the wads for muzzle loading rifles, cut larger holes up to 2in (50mm) in diameter. If you search hard enough you would probably find larger ones. These are normally identified by diameter size.

Crew Punch (Slot Punch)

These are used to cut the slots (crew holes) in straps to accommodate the tongues of the buckles, and they also come in varying sizes. Choice of the correct size in relation to the buckle being used is important. Too small and the crew will not sit snug against the tongue of the buckle while too large allows the buckle to move about.

There are two schools of thought as to how to determine the correct size of crew punch. One is to use the crew punch with the same width as the strap it is to be used on. Unfortunately not all buckles are the same, so while being a good starting point it is not always accurate. A better method is to offer the buckle tongue up to the crew punch and judge how the leather will wrap around the tongue; this does take a little practice.

Trace end punches are basically very large crew punches and are generally used in the saddlery trade for the manufacture of horse harness.

(LEFT) Oval and round punches; *(RIGHT)* Stitch marker, crew punch, egg point chisel; the lead block is used to protect the punches.

RIGHT:
Selecting the correct size of crew punch: If correct, the slot will fit snugly around the buckle tongue.

LEFT:
Selecting the correct size of crew punch: If too small, there would not be enough room for the slot to wrap around the buckle tongue.

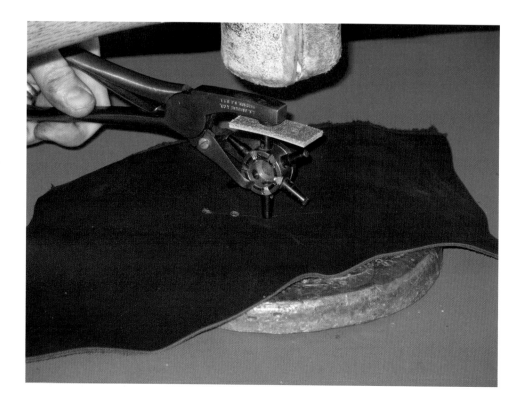

Reaching for inaccessible holes with the punch pliers.

CREW HOLES 'ON THE CHEAP'

If you are on a budget, crew holes can be cut by using the following method. Punch two holes where the crew is to be cut – the distance between the holes will be the size of the desired crew hole. Using the scratch awl and a ruler join the outer edges of the holes with a line, then carefully cut out the leather. Tidy the edges of the crew using sandpaper or a small file. It is very difficult to get the crew hole as neat as a punch, so if you are planning to make a lot of straps or belts a couple of crew punches will prove invaluable.

Strap End Punch

These types of punches are available in varying widths with either pointed (sometimes referred to as egg points or church windows) or rounded ends. They are used to give the ends of straps a professional finish. They are also useful when stitching two pieces of leather together, since a rounded stitch line can be achieved as opposed to two straight ones.

PUNCHING

Punching is a straightforward operation, but there are a few guidelines to observe. To protect the cutting end of your punches always punch into a soft material such as a lead block or piece of wood; it is preferable to punch into the loose grain ends of wood, but if this surface is very rough the underside of the work may need to be protected by placing a piece of scrap leather under it.

Punch over a supported area; unsupported areas give with the impact, causing unwanted movement. Never use metal faced hammers, which will mushroom the ends of the punches and can fracture the metal of cheaper punches. Always use soft faced mallets.

Single punches are held at 90 degrees to the leather, then struck with a mallet. Many beginners will stand square on to the punch, which cramps the arm movement, and they strike the punch tentatively, presumably because of the fear of missing and hitting their hand. Position your body slightly left of the punch, holding it at 90 degrees to the leather surface. Keeping a firm grip strike it square, or you may find it flying across the room. Be confident – the more you think about missing the more likely it is to happen. A couple of good sharp blows should be sufficient to drive the punch through.

With strap end punches ensure that the centre of the punch is lined up with the centre of the strap.

If you are using punch pliers, simply select the required size, place on the desired position and squeeze the handles together. A quick twist of the wrist helps to free the waste material. With a revolving punch, if you are unable to reach the required position of the hole, set the required punch size opposite to its normal position, turn the punch upside down and squeeze the jaws together; place the punch on the leather and knock it through with a mallet.

Mallets and Hammers

Soft faced mallets will help to prevent damage to the ends of your punches and stamps. Wood, rawhide or the better quality nylon mallets are all suitable. However, avoid rubber mallets as they tend to bounce. Choose a reasonable weight mallet, as a lot of effort can be expended when trying to use a very light one.

The face of the harness hammer is domed so that it does not mark the leather surface. It is used for flattening stitching and blocking up keepers (loops). The tack hammer, as the name implies, is for driving in tacks.

Everybody thinks they know how to use a mallet or hammer; you pick it up by the handle and strike the intended object with the face. For some reason beginners tend to strangle these tools – that is, to hold them halfway up the handle. The handles are there for a reason: holding the end of the handle allows the weight of the tool do the work.

BASIC TOOLS CHECKLIST

1. Awl
2. Stitching Clams
3. Stitch Markers
4. Needles
5. Threads
6. Beeswax
7. Pliers
8. Small scissors
9. Round knife (or craft knife) and cutting mat
10. Punch
11. Mallet/hammer
12. Ruler and long straight edge
13. Sharpening stone

Strap Cutting Tools

The purpose of all these tools is to cut straps at a given width. Each has a guide, which runs along a gauge marked in inches and/or centimetres, and a cutting blade. The gauges on these tools are generally not very accurate, so always check the width setting with a ruler. Although it is possible to cut straps using a straight edge and a knife, if you envisage cutting a lot of straps then one of these tools is essential and it will pay for itself in time saved.

Plough Gauge

The plough gauge is the traditional tool used by saddlers. The knife is removable and may need setting up before initial use, as with the round knife.

To use the plough gauge, set the guide to the desired width. Push the knife into the leather keeping the guide tight against the edge of the leather. Continue cutting until there is enough of the strap cut so that you can grasp it. Change position: grasp the strap in the left hand and the knife in the right. Ensuring that the guide is kept tight against the edge, push the knife and lightly pull the leather and work your way along the whole length of the strap. I may be wrong, but I have never seen a left handed plough gauge so all you lefties will have to try to adapt if using this tool.

Draw Gauge

The draw gauge has a removable blade, and while replacements can be purchased, sharpening them is straightforward. Set the guide to required width and hold it against the edge of the leather. Pull the gauge towards you along the length of the hide. Initially the draw gauge can be awkward to use and takes a little practice. The leather tends to ride up the blade, and it is difficult to keep the guide tight against the edge. Holding the leather down behind the blade with your free hand will help alleviate some of the problems.

Strap Cutter

To use the strap cutter set the guide to the desired width, place it tight against the leather and pull it toward you. Keeping the guide against the edge continue down the length of

USING THE PLOUGH GAUGE

Push the tool into the leather to start the cut.

Grasp the end of the strip and push the tool while pulling the strip to complete the cut.

Using the strap cutter.
Pull the tool towards you.

the hide. Most people find the strap cutter easier to use than the draw gauge or plough gauge and it is perfect for cutting very narrow strips. While it does struggle on very heavy leathers, overall it is an ideal tool for the hobbyist.

The blade in the strap cutter is a small razor type blade, which is disposable. To change the blade loosen the two screws on the front, place a round or clickers awl or similar tool into the hole in the middle of the blade and slide it to one side. Take the new blade and push it through the slit in the side – this will push the old blade out. Carefully remove the old blade (for safety grasp it with a pair of pliers), then centre the new blade using the hole, making sure that it is resting on the bottom of the slits. Tighten the screws and you are ready to go.

SAFETY

Always keep the blades sharp, as blunt blades will rip the leather causing the leather fibres on the edge to 'fluff up', while a sharp blade will produce a clean edge. When using the plough gauge keep a firm grasp on the handle. Occasionally on a hide of leather there are patches that are more difficult to cut. If you are not concentrating and you hit one of these patches your hand could slip off the handle and shoot over the blade. The top of the plough gauge knife is sharp and will cause a nasty injury. I speak from experience as one of the worst cuts I have received happened in this manner. For safety's sake the sharp top edge of my plough gauge knife has now been ground blunt.

Shaving Tools

Edge Shaves (Bevellers)

When leather is cut the edges can be very sharp, so the edge shaves (also known as bevellers) are used to remove these edges. Removing the edges also gives the project a more professional look. They are numbered 1 to 6 (the higher the number the more of the edge is removed) and have either a flat or concave back. The concaved backed edge shaves are known as hollow ground. Hollow ground edge shaves are slightly more expensive but give a better finish and are easier to use.

Working clockwise from 12 o'clock: plough gauge, skiver, edge shave, safety beveller, skirt shave.

A No. 2 hollow ground edge shave would be sufficient for all but the heaviest of leathers.

HANDLING

With the leather flat on the work surface place the edge shave on the edge to be removed at an angle of 45 degrees. Push the shave away from you, supporting the work with your free hand, and the leather should come off in one continuous strip. Concentrate on keeping the angle and depth of the shave constant, and keep the free hand away from the front of the tool.

Skirt Shaves

These have a much broader face than the edge shaves; unlike edge shaves they are used to skive (thin down, *see* Chapter 3) the leather edges. They are mainly used by saddlers to skive the inside edges of saddle skirts, hence the name. A raised effect can be achieved on lined items (an item made with a double thickness) by skiving the flesh edges of both parts, and they can also be used to produce an angled edge.

HANDLING

These are used in the same manner as the edge shaves except that a wider shaving is removed, and the angle at which the tool is held will depend on the thickness of leather to be left on the edge.

CAUTION

Ask any saddler to pick out the scariest tool in the workshop and the skirt shave is the one they will choose. It is a very difficult tool to master. Slip and stab yourself with an edge shave and the worst that will happen is that it will hurt and you may get a small cut. Doing the same thing with a skirt shave will cause serious injury. Always be aware of where your free hand is.

Skivers

These tools are used to shave down the thickness of the leather. Their use will be discussed in Chapter 3: Basic Techniques.

Line Marking Tools

Dividers

A good pair of dividers will pay for themselves in the time that they save. Lines running parallel to the leather's edge at a set distance can easily be marked by running one of the legs against the edge. Walking the dividers along the leather will mark the position for punched holes quickly and accurately.

Groovers and Races

These tools are used to cut a groove in the surface of the leather and come in many forms. Some have an adjustable guide which is run along the edge of the leather while others are used free hand. The resulting groove can be used purely as decoration or to stitch into so that the stitching lies below the surface of the leather thus reducing wear. They are also used when folding heavier leathers as a groove placed on the fold line makes folding easier.

Use of these tools is fairly straightforward. Adjustable types are set to the desired distance then, keeping the guide against the edge of the leather, draw the tool towards you while exerting pressure on the cutting edge.

The method of using free hand types will depend on their design and all are easily mastered.

Creases

Creases are used to make an impression in the surface of the leather. They come in many forms; the most commonly used are the screw crease, single crease, and checker.

Screw Crease

The screw crease has two blades held apart by a screw. Adjustment of this screw will increase or decrease the distance between the blades. The blade on the screw side is run against the edge of the leather, which allows a straight line to be made with the inner blade. Although the screw crease can be used as it comes from the manufacturer, a little time spent making a few adjustments will make it easier to use.

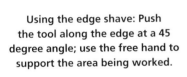

Using the edge shave: Push the tool along the edge at a 45 degree angle; use the free hand to support the area being worked.

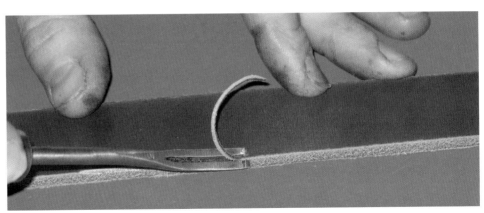

(LEFT TO RIGHT) Checker, dividers, single crease, screw crease, bottom, groover.

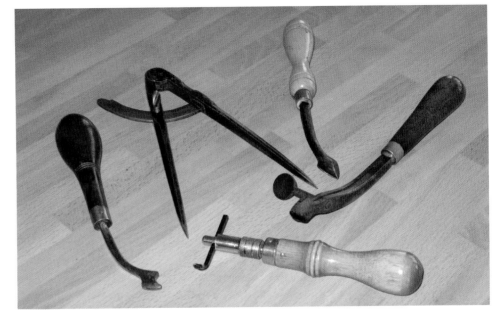

Using the groover. Pull the groover towards you while supporting the work with the free hand.

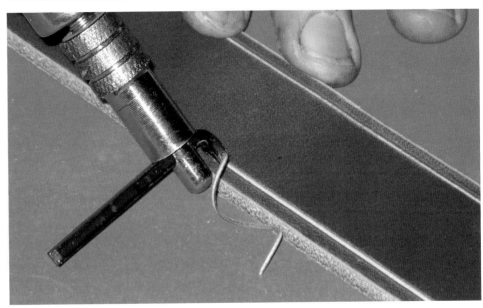

The pattern produced by the checker.

Initial Setup of Screw Crease

When new both blades are of equal length, reducing the inner blade (the blade opposite the screw head) by approximately $1/32$ in (0.75mm) will make it easier to keep the outer blade (the blade with the screw head) against the edge of the leather. Do not reduce it by any more than this amount.

To do this, open the screw to its maximum, place the crease in a vice and carefully file down the inner blade, making sure that the curve of the blade is followed. When the desired amount has been removed, if the end of the blade is too thick, reduce the thickness by filing the outside face following the angle of the bevel. Finally, use the wet and dry emery paper to polish the blade edge until it runs smoothly along the leather. The edge should be thin and round, not sharp.

Single Crease

The single crease has a single blade and can be use anywhere on the leather surface. When new try it on a scrap piece of leather, and polish as described if necessary.

Checkers

This is not a line drawing tool in the strictest sense but has been included as it is used in the same manner as the single and screw crease. These tools have two narrow parallel blades set at a fixed distance and are used for decoration. Saddlers making horse harnesses employ this tool to create the checked patterns on box loops, and the same method can be utilized to great effect on wide belt loops.

HANDLING

All types of creases are used in the same manner and can be used cold. However a more permanent impression can be achieved if they are heated. They need to be heated enough to give a good impression but not enough to burn the leather. There are many factors involve in establishing how long the crease requires heating before it gets to the correct temperature (type of crease, room temperature, strength of heat source, etc.). Quite a bit of practice is required, as burns on the leather will ruin your project.

CREASING

Heat the crease taking care not to get it too hot.

Place the outside blade against the edge and work towards you.

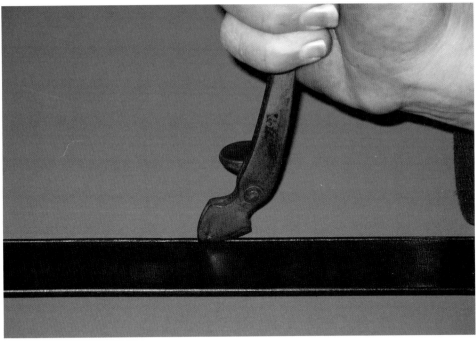

The heat source can be anything from a Bunsen burner to a blow torch on a low setting. Hold the crease like a dagger and use the flat of the blade not the point, as this digs into the leather possibly scarring the surface. Once applied to the leather keep the crease moving – if you pause in one place too long you may burn the leather.

On long runs the crease will periodically need re-heating. Gauging the best time to do this and how much re-heating is required come down to experience and practice.

SAFETY

Safety using creases is really common sense, but it is worth reiterating a few obvious points. You will be working with a naked flame, so ensure that it is placed on a stable platform; ensure that long hair and loose clothing are secured so that there is no possibility of them catching the flame; and turn off the flame immediately upon completion. Remember that the crease is hot; be careful where you put it down and make sure you pick up the correct end.

Splitting machine: rolling block and loop sticks.

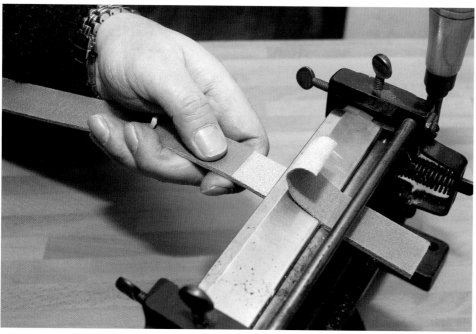

Although expensive, the splitting machine is a very useful tool for reducing leather substance.

Other Tools

Splitting Machine

If you are splitting a lot of leather then this tool is a must. However the down side is that it is very expensive. In my workshop it pays for itself, as we make a lot of items that require keepers made from leather that has been split to approximately half its original thickness. It is also useful when skiving long lengths of leather.

Place the leather between the blade and the roller, and adjust the depth of the cut. Take hold of the leather and pull, which results in a layer of leather being shaved off. For this machine to work efficiently and to prevent the leather from stretching, the blades need to be kept razor sharp.

Loop Sticks

These are use to block up keepers (loops) on straps. Although not essential they give the project a more professional finish. They are made from hard wood, plastic or metal and come in a range of width sizes $^3/_8$–$1^1/_2$in (10–37mm). They can be purchased as a set or individually. You can place two sticks side by side to give a different width, for example placing a $^1/_2$in (12mm) and a $^3/_4$in (19mm) stick together would give a width of $1^1/_4$in (31mm).

Rolling Blocks

These are used for rolled or raised work. They are made from a block of hard wood with grooves of varying widths cut into the surface. The strap is placed into the appropriate groove and tapped into shape.

Measuring and Straight Edges

Having some form of measuring implement is essential. The minimum requirement is a 12in (305mm) ruler marked in inches and centimetres (metal rulers are best as there is less chance of damaging the edge) and a steel tape measure for measuring longer lengths. Small 6in (152mm) metal rulers make a handy addition.

Another useful item to have in the workshop is an 8–10ft (2.5–3m) straight edge. (extremely useful for marking along the length of leather hides). Avoid using wood as it tends to warp if it is not stored correctly.

Small set squares can be purchased at any good DIY store and can prove invaluable when marking right angles.

Care and Storage

Having invested a reasonable amount of your hard earned cash in tools, a little care and maintenance will ensure a prolonged and productive life.

Tools kept in boxes or drawers are liable to knock against each other causing sharpened blades to lose their edges, and rooting around for tools increases the risk of cut fingers. A tool board allows quick access and keeps the tools separate. If space is at a premium a purpose built tool box is not too difficult to assemble. Any design will do, so long as instruments with sharp edges are kept separate. I am convinced that every workshop has a needle gremlin whose sole purpose is to steal needles, so to avert his activities stick a piece of foam to the tool board or box and use it to store the needles.

Use the tools for the purpose that they were intended, and when using knives cut onto a cutting board or mat. Only use soft faced mallets on punches, stamps etc, and punch onto a soft surface ensuring that it is placed on a solid surface.

Sharpening

I cannot emphasize enough the importance of keeping knives sharp. Blunt knives cause accidents. A good habit to adopt is to strop your knife before starting any cutting; this will keep the edge finely honed and should be all that is required to keep the blade in good order. All too frequently knives are left until they are incapable of cutting butter, let alone leather. Knives in this condition will require sharpening on an oil stone before the edge is finely honed. Sharpening any knife takes a little practice and it is easy to ruin an edge, but patience and attention to detail is the key.

There are many forms of sharpening stones on the market. As the method of sharpening on most of them is the same I have only described the use of the oil stone, but the choice as to which you use is yours. Always check the manufacturer's instructions as to the type of lubrication to use on the stone. Some, such as diamond stones, use water as a lubricant and can be ruined if oil is used.

BLADE ANGLES

The angle used to sharpen the blade edge is one of the factors that affect how long a blade will maintain its sharpness. A blade with a steep angle will stay sharper for longer – for example scissors have very steep angles. A narrower angle, however, allows for a sharper edge but the blade will require frequent sharpening.

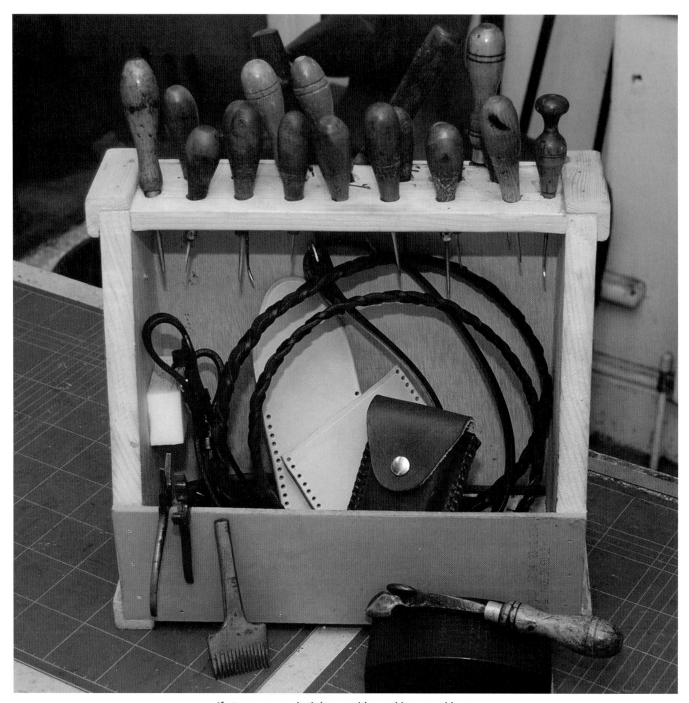

If storage space is tight, consider making a tool box.

USING AN OIL STONE

Use a good quality flat oil stone. To help prevent damage to the surface it is a good idea to either buy a purpose made box for it or make one. Most have one side finer than the other. Always use the finer side, and ensure that it is fixed to the bench. Liberally cover the surface with oil, then following the existing angle of the knife edge place it on the stone and push it back and forth along the length of the stone, maintaining pressure on the blade and ensuring that the whole length of the blade is sharpened equally. Do not let the stone dry out; add more oil as required. When a thin metal shaving (swarf) forms, turn the blade over and sharpen the other side. The swarf is sometimes visible, but often it is only apparent to touch. With a light touch, move the thumb over the edge, not into the edge; the swarf will feel like a ridge along the edge of the blade. Once complete strop the knife to remove the remaining swarf and to hone and polish the edge.

SAFETY TIPS

Making a strop and using it for the first few times can be a messy business, so covering the work surface before starting would be a wise precaution. Carborundum powder contains fine metal filings so it is a good idea to use gloves and to wash your hands immediately you have finished (be careful not to rub your eyes until you have done this).

USING THE STROP

Remember that the strop is not used to sharpen blades that are extremely dull but merely to hone and polish the blades to a razor-like finish.

There are two ways in which the strop can be used. The first method, and probably the easier method for beginners, is to start by laying the strop flat on the bench. To stop it from slipping either tack it to the bench through the hole in the handle or place the edge against a fixed object. Following the angle of the blade, place it on the grinding surface and draw it toward you. (Do not push the blade back and forth like you would on an oil stone; the blade would cut into the surface on the forward stroke.) Repeat this process working along the length of the blade five or six times, then turn the blade over and work on other side. When the blade has a good edge, flip the strop over and work the blade in the same manner against the plain side to remove any residue.

The second method is to hold the strop by the handle either flat on the bench or at an angle. Place the blade on the top end of the grinding surface (the end nearest the handle) and draw the blade down the length of the strop. When you reach the bottom of the strop, flip the blade over and draw it back to the top. Keep repeating this process while working along the length of the blade, then work the blade against the plain side of the strop. This sounds more complicated in writing than it is in practice. The movement that you are trying to achieve is the same as a barber in the western movies stropping his razor. Exercise care when stropping round knives using this method. The design of the round knife means that it effectively has a blade edge on either side and it is very easy to run it into your hand on the up stroke.

Occasionally the strop will need recharging; simply sprinkle a little carborundum powder onto the grinding surface and use the sharpening action of the blade to work the powder into the surface. Unless the strop has been left for long periods in the sun they rarely need recharging with tallow. Sometimes, especially when the strops are new, working the blades against the plain surface of the strop is not enough to remove the residue. In this situation the careful use of a cloth or kitchen paper with a drop of methylated spirit or lighter fuel works wonders.

SHARPENING EDGE SHAVES

Edge shaves and skirt shaves also require occasional sharpening. Sharpening these on the backside only will be sufficient. You can work skirt and flat backed edge shaves on the strop, then use a thin piece of leather to clear the accumulated debris from the middle. Hollow ground shaves require a little more attention as care must be taken not to flatten the curved back. The edge of the strop can be used, but it is better to use a slip stone as the thin end will fit into the hollow.

The Workshop

The beauty of leatherwork is that with a little ingenuity and care it can be done almost anywhere. However a dedicated work bench does make life easier. Ideally it should be free standing allowing access to at least three sides and large enough to accommodate a leather hide when laid out. The surface area should be 8ft (2.5m) long and a minimum of 3ft (1m) wide, and the height should allow you to work comfortably on items while standing without having to bend too far over. Obviously space available will dictate the actual sizes,

TOOL CARE

Making a Strop

This is not the only method of making a strop. This is the one that I use, and students on my training courses seem to like it. Do not worry if your dimensions differ or you do not wish to cut a handle – the choice is yours.

To make the strop you will require a piece of suitable wood or board; any type will do but for rigidity it needs to have an approximate thickness of ³/₈in (10mm) or more. Also required are two pieces of leather to cover the front and back of the cut wood (use a cheap cut of leather – natural vegetable tanned leather is best), tallow, carborundum powder and a good quality adhesive such as Evo-Stik. Carborundum powder can be purchased from artist suppliers and comes in various grades. A grade of 120 grit will suffice, but for if you require a finer strop use a grade of 180 grit. Tallow is an animal fat and can be difficult to source. A search on the internet should produce a supplier, but lard could be used if necessary.

Cut your wood to the dimensions given. Then cut two pieces of leather to fit the rectangular part of the strop. A hole drilled into the handle will facilitate the use of a thong which will allow the strop to be hung out of the way when not in use. With coarse sandpaper rough the grain surfaces of both pieces of leather (the best side) – this will be the side that will be stuck to the strop – and both faces of the wood. This will give the adhesive a better surface to adhere to. Using the adhesive in accordance with the manufacturer's instructions stick the leather onto the strop; the flesh side (worst side) of the leather on both sides of the strop should be showing.

Take the tallow and rub it into the surface of the leather (only do one side of the strop, not both) ensuring that the whole surface is liberally covered. Sprinkle a small amount of carborundum powder over the surface, then rub it into the tallow (do not be too heavy handed with the carborundum powder as a little will go a long way). Repeat this process until a good base has been built up over the entire surface. This surface is used to grind the blade (the grinding surface); the other surface is used to remove any tallow and powder that has accumulated on the blade and to keep the blade 'keen'. Finally, tap the strop on the bench to remove any excess powder, and it is then ready for use.

Suggested dimensions for a strop.

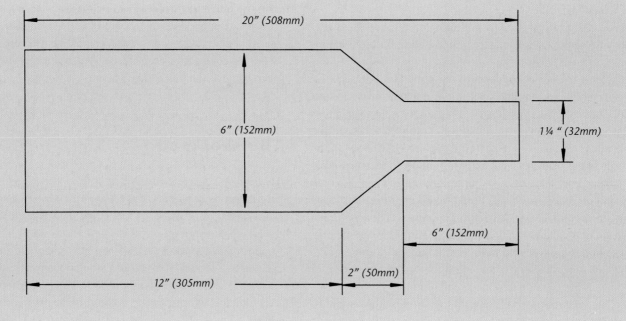

and the chances are that the bench will probably be built against a wall, but try to make it as long and wide as possible, as cutting leather on the floor is awkward and leads to mistakes and damaged floor coverings. A foot rail placed at a suitable height will make long periods sitting at the bench more comfortable, and a loop fastened to the side of the bench makes a handy storage place for your stitching clams.

If you are using a tool board, organize it so that all tools of the same type are together and mount it within easy reach of the bench ensuring that any protruding blades are safely positioned. Over a period of time you will find that you will accumulate a variety of buckles and hardware. Keep your old coffee jars and use them for storage – this allows you to see what you have without having to open a multitude of tins. Maintain a small notebook for re-ordering, or better still have a small white board positioned close to your buckles. As you run out of an item write it down; then when you come to place your order everything is to hand.

Workshop Safety

It is not the intention here to give a long list of health and safety rules. However, whether working in a dedicated workshop or on the dining room table you should always be safety conscious. Little things could avert a potential accident, like putting tools away after use; labelling any liquids clearly and replacing lids immediately after use; placing waste sharp implements such as spent Stanley knife blades in a sealed container (empty drinks cans are ideal for this); keeping the floor space swept and free from obstructions (it is amazing how slippery a leather scrap can be on a hard floor surface); and storing everything out of the reach of children. Any electrical cables should be placed along the sides of walls and protected – a sharp knife dropped onto a cable will slice through the insulation.

It is not a good idea to wear open-toed sandals or to have bare feet when working with sharp implements. Long hair and loose clothing should be tied back when working around naked flames or machinery. Try to keep the work surface as free of clutter as possible, and store away tools and liquids after use (we only have one pair of hands and can only use one tool at a time). Adults and children alike cannot resist the temptation to play with any sharp implement left out, stabbing them into the bench or, worse still, into the first piece of leather they see which may well be part of your project.

When concentrating on the task in hand it is easy to become blinkered and lose track of your surroundings. Occasionally glance around so at least you are aware if little Jimmy has decided to tie your shoe laces together or the dog has lain down behind your feet. All this is really common sense and most people will employ these practices without realizing it.

Making a Lead Block

Using a lead block for punching is preferable to using pieces of wood, as the face can be hammered flat or re-melted when it becomes pitted with use. Making a lead block is a simple task, as lead melts at low temperatures and the process can be carried out on the cooker or on a camping stove.

There are a few safety issues to consider before commencing. As it is melting lead gives off poisonous gases, so the room must be well ventilated. Better still do it outside, avoid breathing the fumes and wear a mask. Lead is extremely heavy so make sure that the heat source can support the weight. Lead may melt at low temperatures, but it will still burn human flesh. Any implement used for the process cannot be used again for cooking.

You will need something to melt the lead in and an old spoon. I use a small frying pan, with a blow torch as the heat source. Lead can be obtained from a builders' merchants, but it is cheaper to try to obtain scrap lead – try talking nicely to your local roofer. Cut the lead into small pieces. Place the pan on the heat source and add a few pieces of lead. As the lead melts keep adding more pieces until the desired depth is achieved – approximately 1in (25mm) should be sufficient. Use the spoon to skim off any scum that forms on the surface. Turn off the heat and stir it well to release any trapped gases (these can form holes on the surface), and then leave it to cool. Do not try to move the pan using the handle, as it will not support the weight. The block does not stick to the pan (because of the different types of metals and melting temperatures) and can be easily removed by tipping the pan. Wash the surfaces with washing-up liquid to remove any carbon build-up, and your lead block is ready to use.

Soft panel hides stored in the warehouse at Abbey Saddlery and Crafts Ltd, Knutsford.

CHAPTER 2

LEATHER

Leather is an expensive commodity, and so a basic understanding of the tanning process, properties of different leathers, how it is sold and the various terms used in the trade will hopefully save some costly mistakes when buying your leather.

The definition of leather given in the Oxford Dictionary is *Skin prepared for use by tanning or similar process*. This gives the leatherworker a vast array of leathers to choose from. Cowhides are the most frequently used, but calf, sheep, goat, pig and deer are also quite common. There are then more exotic leathers such as snake, horse, elephant, lizard, shark and crocodile. Whilst I have no problem using leather processed from domestic farmed or culled animals, I will not use the latter types as I feel that they look better on their original owners.

Leather has a two-layer construction. The surface on which the hair grew is known as the *grain* layer, which is relatively thin in comparison to the thickness of the skin. Once tanned with the hair removed it has a smooth finish. In any discussion of leather, reference to the 'grain' means the top surface, generally the best side of the leather. The grain layer merges into a thicker fibrous layer which lies next to the flesh of the animal, hence the underside of the skin is known as the *flesh* side, which is rougher than the grain and is sometimes fluffy with a suede effect; its actual finish will depend on the split of the leather and how it has been processed. The condition of the fibrous layer – the density, amount of filling with oils and fats during tanning – determines the quality of the leather.

The initial substance (thickness) of the skin will depend on the age of the animal at the time of slaughter.

Structure

Skin is an amazing piece of engineering. Nature has designed it to be self-healing and porous so that it breathes; yet to keep us from becoming waterlogged whenever it rains, naturally occurring oils make it waterproof. Maintaining these properties through the process of tanning gives leather its unique qualities.

Preserving the Hide

The process of preserving leather is called tanning. The majority of leather in modern times is either vegetable tanned or mineral tanned, which is commonly known as chrome tanning due to the chromium salts used in the process. The actual tanning procedure is roughly the same for both; the difference is in the type of preserving solutions employed.

Leather layers.

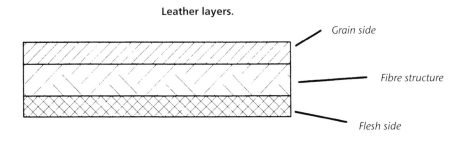

Grain side

Fibre structure

Flesh side

Vegetable Tanning

Tannin, a substance that occurs naturally in the bark, leaves and seedpods of trees, is the preserving solution used in vegetable tanning. For many centuries in Britain oak bark was the main source of tannin. Although still in use, tanneries now tend to use tannin from a variety of barks. Vegetable tanning is quite a long process and can take up to four months, with some forms of vegetable tanning taking even longer. The resultant leather is stiffer than leather that has been mineral tanned and will absorb water. This makes it ideal for carving, stamping and moulding.

Mineral Tanning (Chrome Tanning)

Mineral tanning uses mineral salts as the preserving solution, the main one being chromium salts. These salts penetrate the hides quickly, and the actual tanning process can be completed in a day. The resultant hides are softer and more flexible then vegetable tanned hides and they are water resistant, making them ideal for clothing, bags and shoes, but they cannot be used for stamping, carving and moulding. Mineral tanned hides can be recognized by their blue green colour. On dyed hides this can be seen in the centre layer when the hide is cut.

The Tanning Process

Preparing hides for tanning begins with a process known as curing. To prevent decay this must be carried out immediately the skin is removed from the animal, so it is normally done at the abattoir. There are various methods of curing. Wet salting is where the hides are covered in salt, stacked into piles and left for approximately thirty days. A quicker method is brine curing, where the hides are agitated in a salt water bath for twelve to sixteen hours. Other methods of curing involve drying the hides or storing them at low temperatures.

Next the salt is removed from the hides by soaking them in clean water followed by a further soaking in lime pits to loosen the hair. The majority of hair is then removed by machine, with any remaining hair, flesh and fat being removed by hand, a process known as scudding. Further washing removes the lime. The next step, known as pickling, is where the actual tanning process takes place.

In vegetable tanning the hides are soaked in a series of vats. If the hide was placed directly into a full strength solution, the outside of the hide would be tanned quickly, preventing any penetration to its centre. To avoid this, the hides are moved through a series of vats where the solution strength is progressively increased. In mineral tanning the hides are placed in drums to which the chromium salts are slowly added until it is at the required strength.

The actual tanning process is now complete, and after any excess tanning solution is removed the hide goes through the finishing processes. These include splitting to desired thickness, dyeing, fat liquoring to replace natural oils lost during tanning, smoothing and stretching, buffing to cover any imperfections on the hide and embossing. Traditionally the finishing processes are known as currying, which is a highly skilled job – a mistake at this stage could ruin months of work. The final stage is measuring and grading. Not all leathers will go through all of these processes.

The currying requirements will differ for individual trades within the leather industry, hence many tanneries do not curry their own hides; instead they are sold to specialist curriers who will prepare the hides in accordance with each specialty. An example of this is J & E Sedgwick & Co, who produce high quality hides for the equestrian trade, while other curriers may specialize in upholstery, shoe or clothing leathers.

Oil Tanning

Oil tanning is one of the oldest methods of tanning, and although still employed its use is limited. It was the method used by the North American Indians. The women would scrape the hides clean of hair and flesh, then alternately soak them and rub them with grease made from the animal's brain and liver. This process would be repeated until the leather when dried was as soft as a piece of cloth.

Today, up to the pickling stage, the hides are prepared in the same way as mineral and vegetable tanning. Then, instead of being placed into pickling vats or drums, oil (the commonest being cod liver oil) is forced into the wet hides.

Leather Terms

Every industry will have its own mystical terms, and the leather trade, being an old established industry, probably has more than most. This section will explain how these terms are conceived so you can knowingly nod when confronted by a leather catalogue or at the warehouse making your first purchase.

Basic Terms

■ **Hide** Leather from larger animals, such as cow hide, horsehide.

■ **Skin** Leather from smaller animals, such as sheep skin goatskin, pigskin, calfskin.

■ **Runoff** The place where the fibre structure of the hide starts to noticeably change; these are sometimes referred to as the *soggy ends* and occur at the bellies and shoulders (this term tends to be used more in the saddlery trade where the hide quality is more crucial).

■ **Substance** The thickness of the hide.

■ **Natural vegetable tanned** Leather that has been vegetable tanned but not dyed.

Splits

Leather splits.

Cuts

Thicker hides may be split into two or more layers before they are tanned.

■ **Grain split** The grain layer or top split; generally finished on both grain and flesh surfaces.

■ **Middle split** The middle layer; has a suede finish on both sides.

■ **Flesh split** The flesh layer; has a suede finish on both sides, with the flesh side sometimes having a coarser finish.

Generally it is only cowhides which are divided in this fashion, and each cut will display different qualities and strengths. It is important to understand these differences, especially if your project involves the leather coming under any stress. If you make a pair of horse reins out of the bellies, the rider would probably be left galloping with a broken rein. This would have been avoided if a vegetable tanned back of 4mm to 4.5mm in thickness had been used.

■ **Bellies** Have a very loose fibre structure, are very stretchy with little tensile strength, and have a spongy feel when compressed between the thumb and forefinger; these attributes make them unsuitable for most leatherwork projects.

Different coloured bridle butts.

How hides are cut.

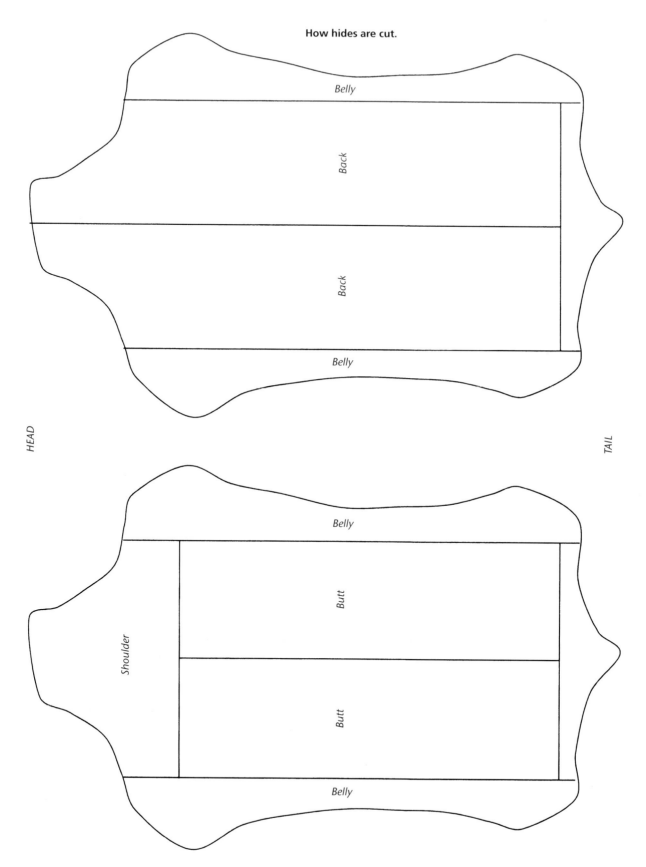

HEAD

TAIL

- **Shoulders** Much better fibre structure than the bellies but the hide can be uneven especially as it runs off toward the neck; the quality of shoulders can vary greatly, but good quality shoulders are suitable for most leatherworking projects.
- **Butts** The best parts of the hide, where the fibre structure is fairly consistent. The usable length is approximately 50–60in (127–150cm) and the usable width approximately 24–28in (61–70cm).
- **Backs** Basically butts with the shoulders left on: the hides are cut down the whole length of the spine and the bellies removed; backs are only cut from hides with good quality shoulders. The approximate usable length is 70–80in (178–200cm) and the usable width approximately 24–28in (61–70cm). Backs are ideal for making long straps.
- **Half** or **pair** Butts and backs are referred to as half or pair: *half* means the butt or back from one side of the spine and a *pair* means the butts or backs from both sides of the spine.
- **Sides** Like backs, the hide is cut down the whole length of the spine but they differ in that the bellies are left on.
- **Bends** Basically a bend is half a butt; normally refers to sole leather.

Types of Leather

DIFFERENT ANIMALS
As each cut of leather displays different qualities, leather from different animals will also have its own characteristics.

- **Cowhide** Leather from a mature bovine; strictly speaking there is a distinction between leather from cows, cattle, bulls and so on, but as these differences are minor I have used the term cowhide to encompass all bovines. Cowhide and its derivatives are the most common leathers available and can be processed in many forms making them suitable for most leather trades from the fashion industry to saddlery.
- **Sheepskin** Nice soft leather that can be used for clothing, gloves, linings, etc. However, the fibre structure is fairly loose, making it much weaker than cowhide of comparable substance and not as hard wearing.

- **Pigskin** Has a small and compact fibre layer, making it stronger than cowhide of a comparable substance. The grain surface is very distinctive, as the bristle holes, which go right through the skin, are grouped in clumps of three, a characteristic which also makes the skin difficult to waterproof. Care must be taken if using pigskin as a lining, as linings are often glued in place before stitching and if too much glue is used it will seep through to the grain surface.
- **Goatskin** Also has a compact fibre layer which makes it strong soft leather, but unlike pigskin the hairs do not penetrate the skin, thus it is easier to waterproof. Archaeological evidence suggests that goatskin was widely used by the Roman legions for tents, shoes, bags etc. Today it is used for clothing, shoes, gloves, bookbinding. A lovely leather to work.
- **Kangaroo hide** Stronger, more durable, suppler and more water resistant than any of the previously mentioned leathers. Thin but strong, it is favoured by falconers for making jesses and is occasionally used for clothing and high class sporting goods. The superior characteristics that make it such unique leather also make it very expensive. An amazing natural material. (Note: All kangaroo leather originates from freely roaming herds in Australia. No kangaroos are farmed or hunted for commercial purposes. Australia is currently vastly overpopulated with kangaroos, with their numbers steadily increasing. As a result, the Australian government, in conjunction with world environmental and species control associations, has developed a humane species control programme.)

DESCRIPTION OF FINISH

- **Aniline dyed** Leather that has been dyed by immersion in a dye bath with the grain left in its natural state and no application of any pigment finish.
- **Semi-aniline** Aniline leather that has a light pigment finish which gives a degree of resistance to dirt and moisture.
- **Pigment finish** Leather that has had a protective polymer finish containing pigment applied to the grain, giving it greater durability and resistance to marking.
- **Bark tanned** Leather that has been vegetable tanned using the tannins contained in tree bark.

■ **Oak bark tanned**   Bark tanned leather which has been tanned in pits for not less than five to six months with tannin from oak bark being used as the tanning agent.

TYPES OF GRAIN

■ **Full grain**   A grain split or an unsplit hide which has little or no damage to its grain surface and can be used as it is. Leaving the grain in its natural state allows for the best fibre strength, resulting in greater durability. These types of leathers are the best grades available.

■ **Corrected grain**   Any grain split or an unsplit hide that has had its grain surface sanded or buffed to remove any imperfections, with an imitation grain then embossed onto the surface. These types of leather are inferior in quality to full grain leathers.

■ **Top grain**   This is a rather confusing term. While checking facts for this book I found many conflicting definitions. The definition given by the *Glossary of Leather Terms*, published by the International Council of Tanners in 1968, states that it is a North American term used to describe the grain split of a hide, which confirms my own understanding.

PATTERN/COLOUR

■ **Embossed leather**   Leather that has the grain surface embossed with a pattern imitating or resembling the grain pattern of some animal.

■ **Morocco**   Vegetable tanned goatskin with the characteristic grain pattern developed naturally or by hand boarding or graining only.

■ **Shrunken grain**   Leather that has been specially tanned so as to shrink the grain layer producing a grain surface of uneven folds and valleys, sometimes referred to as *drawn leather.*

■ **Russet or tooling leather**   Vegetable tanned cowhide which has not been dyed; has a flesh pink colour and is ideal for stamping, dying, carving and moulding.

■ **Latigo**   Leather that has been tanned with aluminium salts and gambier (an astringent extract of Eastern plant), normally yellow in colour with a waxy feel.

STRONG LEATHERS

■ **Rawhide**   Leather that has not gone through the tanning process: the hide is cleaned, then stretched on a frame and left to dry; very strong – one of its uses is to make lacing.

■ **Sole leather**   Vegetable tanned leather sold as bends and mainly used for shoe soles; it is possible to mould the thinner bends, but beware, sole leather is very difficult to cut.

SOFT LEATHERS

■ **Cowhide split**   Normally the middle or flesh split, which has a suede finish on both sides.

■ **Buckskin**   Oil tanned leather made from deerskin, strictly speaking; very soft and supple, making it ideal for clothing.

■ **Kip**   Leather from a young or immature cow; used for clothing, bags and linings.

■ **Calf**   Leather from an immature bovine; very soft and used extensively in the fashion industry. [Note: The distinction between *kip* and *calf* is a bit confusing. *Kip* is made from larger calves giving an average skin size of approx 15–25sq ft (1.4–2.4m^2). Calf skins are 5–10 sq ft (0.5–1m^2).]

■ **Suede**   Middle or flesh split leather with velvet-like texture. The term comes from the French phrase *Gants de Suède*, meaning 'Gloves of Sweden', and Swedish glove leather is usually made from lambskins tanned with willow bark, making them very soft and warm.

■ **Nubuck**   A full grain or grain split leather that has been buffed on the grain side to produce suede-like finish; occasionally the flesh side is also buffed. It differs from suede in that it has a finer texture and is thicker and stronger. One of its uses is in high quality shoes and boots.

■ **Doeskin**   Very soft leather, originally made from a female deer, but today normally made from the flesh split of lamb or sheep and sometimes goat; usually white or cream, and used for gloves and linings.

■ **Nappa**   Full grain sheepskin, and may also be made from goat or kid; soft and supple, so suited for clothing, gloves, etc.

- **Skiver** Grain split of sheep or lambskin, and can sometimes refer to goatskin; produces very thin leather that is used for linings and book binding.
- **Parchment** Generally the flesh split of sheepskin, but can also be made from ass or goatskin; translucent or opaque with a smooth surface, so suitable for writing or book binding.
- **Chamois** The flesh split of sheep or lambskins which has been oil tanned; very soft leather that may be used for linings and some clothing (and probably familiar to car owners for leathering off the car after it has been washed).
- **Pig suede** Flesh split of pigskin; can be use for smaller leather goods, but more often used for linings.

SPECIAL FINISHES

- **Retanned** Leather that has gone through the tanning process twice, normally vegetable and then mineral tanning, which gives a leather that has characteristics in between vegetable tanned leather and mineral tanned leather.
- **Patent leather** A high quality grain split or full grain leather that is given a high gloss flexible finish; originally achieved by using layer upon layer of various daubs, varnishes and lacquers based on linseed oil, but today a plastic coating is normally used.

How Leather is Sold

Hides and skins will come from the tanneries with a square footage marked on them. This denotes the surface area, and the price is given per square foot. The thickness (substance) is given in millimetres. Thicknesses will normally be given in a range (for example, 3–3.5mm or 7–9oz). This is because no two animals are the same, and the thickness of the hides or skins vary slightly across their surface area.

Just to confuse things, many European tanneries are marking hides and skins in square metres. In the USA, some suppliers and tanneries use the term ounces to denote the thickness. This term derives from the approximate weight of one square foot of leather; 1oz equals $1/64$in (0.4mm); therefore, if you multiply $1/64$ by the number of ounces you will get the thickness. For equivalents, 1sq ft equals 0.09m²; 1lb in weight equals 16oz, which in metric equals 0.45 kilos (*see* Appendix for a leather substance table giving the equivalent thicknesses).

Backs, butts, shoulders and sides are normally sold at a fixed price however; shoulders can sometimes be sold by the square footage. Suppliers who specialize in saddlery leather will describe their backs and butts as bridle butts, bridle backs, rein backs, stirrup butts, and so on. These types of leather are high grade, dyed and heavily oiled and are not generally suited for carving or stamping, but they can be moulded. Although these leathers are expensive it is worth keeping them in mind as they can be used to great effect.

Sole leather is sold in a totally different way. It is priced per pound in weight, and the thickness is occasionally given in irons. One iron is equal to $1/48$in (0.5mm).

Leather Quality

Although leather is graded for quality at the tannery, it is always best, where possible, to inspect the leather yourself. It is very difficult to find an unblemished hide or skin. Growth lines and wire marks, caused by cattle rubbing themselves on barbed wire, are frequently found on the grain surface. Growth lines can add to a project providing they are not too pronounced; wire marks can penetrate fairly deep, look ugly and leave a weak spot in the hide. You will need to use your own judgment as to whether the growth lines are acceptable and if you can work around any wire marks without having too much waste.

Squeezing the leather between your fingers will give an indication to its fibre structure. A spongy feel indicates a loose structure and vice versa. The looser the structure, the weaker the tensile strength. When buying backs and butts check the run offs. Sometimes these can extend a fair distance into the hide, which leaves you with a lot of wastage. This is more important if you are making items that require a consistent strength throughout.

Generally, apart from the odd surface blemish, graded hides and skins are fairly constant in quality. However, leather marked with the initials TR, meaning *Tannery Run*, will need closer inspection as they have not been sorted or graded before leaving the tannery.

The warehouse at Abbey Saddlery.

Buying Leather

Do not be put off by all the technical jargon. Buying leather is much easier than it sounds on paper, and at the start of each project in this book there will be a suggestion on the type of leather required. To help you make that first purchase here are a few pointers.

Leather can be purchased from leather retailers, craft shops, leather wholesalers or the tanneries. Today, many of these places have websites and/or catalogues and operate mail order systems. Availability of material sold at each of these outlets will depend on the individuals, but in general:

- **Craft shops** Sell scraps, parts of hides and skins and pre-cut kits.
- **Leather retailers** Sell scraps, hides, whole skins and pre-cut kits; wider choice than craft shops.
- **Leather wholesalers and tanneries** Sell an extensive range of leathers within their speciality; many wholesalers and tanneries specialize in certain types of leather, such as saddlery leathers, upholstery leathers (may have minimum order quantities).

Plan your project and decided what effect you are trying to achieve: for example if you are planning a shopping bag which you would like to roll up when not in use then you would use a soft leather such as suede; if it is to be decorated by carving or stamping then use a russet or tooling hide. If you are unsure, ask. Staff at leather outlets are generally very knowledgeable and more than willing to help. Do not pretend that you know more than you do, as this could lead to costly mistakes.

The quality of the leather you purchase will depend on you, but you do get what you pay for. There is no point in buying a top quality butt just for practice, but bear in mind that working poor quality leather is sometimes more difficult than working better quality leather. You need to strike a happy medium.

Be aware that there are few outlets willing to sell part hides or skins, and the likelihood is you will have to purchase the whole piece. Also, just because leather is sold by the square foot do not expect your hide to come with straight edges and square corners. The machines used to measure hides and skins have included every bit of the surface area, even parts which may be unusable.

Storage and Handling

Storage

It is surprisingly easy to damage the grain side of leather through careless handling or storage. Leather is best stored flat, grain side to grain side; any damage will then be to the flesh side. However, do not store natural vegetable tanned hides with dyed hides; the vegetable tanned hides could absorb any excess dyes and oils.

If there is insufficient space available, roll up the hide loosely with the grain on the inside; if you need to stop the roll from springing apart, tie it with a material that will not mark the leather, such as a piece of ribbon or a strip of cloth. Never use sticky tape as this can mark the surfaces. Also take care not to place heavy objects on the roll, as it may flatten and crease the leather. This is especially relevant for skins which are generally softer.

The storage atmosphere is of equal importance. A cool room free from damp is best. A room with the central heating going full tilt will dry out the leather, making it brittle (more relevant to vegetable tanned and oiled leathers). A damp shed can cause mildew and possibly damage from silverfish. (Silverfish damage manifests itself as irregular patches and grooves in the surface of the leather. This can often be mistaken for rodent damage.)

Handling

If you have ordered your leather via mail order it will arrive rolled and wrapped with some form of packaging. Eagerly you take a knife and run it down the length of the package, tear off the wrappings, only to find a knife cut running across the hide, or at worst, if you have ordered a thin skin it falls open in many pieces. In my experience, leather delivered via mail order is extremely well packaged, and it takes patience and care to open it without damaging the contents.

When laying out your hide check that the work surface is clear, especially if laying the hide grain down. Make it a rule not to place items on the hide and to store away any remaining hide as soon as it is no longer required. Take care not to drag tools across it; this may sound obvious, but it is easy to become complacent especially when using long straight edges.

Squaring hides:
First a straight line is drawn
with a scratch awl.

Squaring hides: The leather is then
cut with the round knife; divid-
ing the back in the middle makes
handling easier.

As already mentioned, natural vegetable tanned leather will absorb dirt and grease easily, so ensure that hands and work surfaces are clean.

SQUARING THE HIDE

At some point you may wish to cut a belt or strap from your hide and for this you will need a straight edge to work from. If your intention is to only make belts and straps, then this will be the first action required. Before starting ensure that your knife is sharp.

Place the straight edge against best edge of the hide, the edge nearest the spine. The spine edge will have a tight fibre structure; the opposite edge will have a looser structure (the soggy end). On top graded hides it is sometimes difficult to distinguish between the two.

With the scratch awl mark a line along the hide. Make the mark as deep as possible and you will find that the blade of the round knife wants to follow the impression. Weights placed on the straight edge will help to prevent slippage, but ensure that the hide is protected when you do this. Using the round knife as described in Chapter 1, carefully cut along the line. It is possible to use a Stanley knife: simply run it along the straight edge, but take care that the straight edge does not slip. When cutting heavier leathers it is easier to make two or more cuts rather than trying to cut through in one.

Another method is to place the straight end along the centre of the hide and divide it into two. As a working Master Saddler this is the method I use, as the majority of my work is a variation on strap work. It makes the hides easier to handle and store. However, if the hide is to be used for a variety of projects then this method is not recommended as you may need the full width of the hide sometime in the future.

ECONOMIC CUTTING AND WASTAGE

Although you are eager to get started, take a few moments to consider how to get the most from the leather. There is always going to be a certain amount of wastage, but this can be reduced by thinking before you act. Leather is unlike fabric; patterns are normally marked on the leather with a scratch awl, and some form of marking has to be made to join pieces together. If these are placed incorrectly the piece is ruined, so always check twice before acting.

Inspect the grain carefully and make a mental note of any imperfections; on the flesh side note the soggy ends. Consider which part of the hide your project will be cut from. If the appearance of the grain surface on the soggy areas is good, and the flesh side is going to be hidden from view and strength is not an issue, maybe these areas could be utilized within this project, leaving the better parts of the hide for future projects.

Place the patterns on the hide and move them about to obtain the most economic position. If the patterns have a straight side, can they be placed together? Then only a single line would have to be cut, saving on wastage and effort.

Keep any usable offcuts in a scrap box. It is surprising how quickly you accumulate offcuts, so separating different colours and types of leather will save time in the future. Offcuts can be used for repairs and smaller projects such as key rings and drinks coasters. Before starting your project it is worth spending a few minutes checking the scrap box, as there may be a suitable piece buried within it.

Mistakes will be made – that is how we learn – but a little time spent planning can help keep these to a minimum.

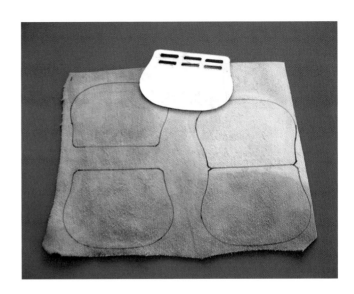

Wasteful positioning of patterns (on the left); efficient positioning the patterns (as shown on the right) reduces wastage; for clarity the leather was marked on the flesh side with a felt-tip marker.

Stitching two edges together using a butt stitch.

CHAPTER 3

BASIC TECHNIQUES

Skiving

Skiving (sometimes referred to as paring) is a process where the edges of the leather are shaved down. It is used at any place where the thickness of the leather needs to be reduced, such as on belts where the leather folds to accommodate the buckle; without skiving it would be too bulky. The aim is to achieve a wedge shape so that the thickness is reduced gradually rather than jumping from one thickness to another. Sometimes the edges of a project are skived to produce a rounded effect.

Normally the flesh side of the leather is skived, but there are occasions where the grain may require skiving (for example, in splicing two pieces of leather together, the flesh would be skived on one piece and the grain on the other so that when joined a continuous thickness is maintained).

Using the Round Knife

Before starting make sure that the knife has been stropped and is sharp. The most common mistake made is to try to push the knife through the leather. Think of a joint of meat. You would not push the carving knife through it, you would slice through it. The same applies when using the round knife – slice, don't push.

1. Place the leather on the bench with the surface to be skived uppermost. Hold the leather in the left hand, positioning it so that it is behind the edge of the bench. Place the round knife on the right edge of the leather approximately ½in (12mm) from the front edge with the blade positioned slightly right of its centre.

2. Drop the left hand slightly so that it does not obstruct the knife. Slightly lift the knife so that the blade is pointing down and push. The curve of the blade will slice into the leather as it goes forward.

3. Continue in the same manner along the width of the leather. Repeat the process until the required amount of skiving is achieved.

4. Any loose fibres can be removed by turning the leather over, laying it flat on the cutting mat, and rolling the blade of the round knife across the front edge of the leather. While performing this manoeuvre, the blade should touch but not cut the leather edge. Using the round knife in this manner requires a lot of practice. Beginners will find it easier to take off a little at a time; people well practised with the round knife tend to take off the whole amount in one clean movement.

Using the Skiver

Skivers are easier to use than the round knife but still require a little practice. Although the designs may differ the handling technique is the same. Before starting make sure that the blade is sharp, replacing it if necessary.

Hold the leather on the bench with the surface to be skived uppermost and pull the tool towards you. The more pressure applied to the tool the deeper the cut; it is better to use a light pressure and remove a little at a time. Remove any loose fibres using the same technique as with the round knife. (Use any sharp knife if a round knife is not available.)

Although it is possible to skive the full width of a strap using the safety edge beveller, these tools are better suited to shaving down the strap edges.

SKIVING WITH THE ROUND KNIFE

Allow the shape of the knife to do the work; push and slice through the leather.

As the knife is pushed forward the shape will naturally take it over to one side.

Skiving should produce a uniform taper.

Safety bevellers are ideal for skiving edges; they are
easier to use than skirt shaves.

Using the skiver: Draw the tool towards you while holding the
leather with the free hand.

Joining Leather

At some point in your leatherworking career you will need to
be able to join two pieces of leather together. There are many
options available, and the method you choose will depend
on the result that you are trying to achieve. However, each
method requires a little practice and a lot of patience in order
to achieve a professional finish.

Riveting

A hole must be punched through both pieces of leather to be
joined. A correctly sized hole is important, as one too large

will allow the leather to move and eventually the rivet may
work loose. It is better to have a slightly smaller hole to ensure
a tight fit. Under strain leather will stretch causing the hole
to enlarge, so this method of joining is not ideal under these
circumstances. Fixing rivets will require the use of a setting
tool consisting of an anvil and setter, which are relatively in-
expensive and readily available.

A mistake made while riveting could ruin your project, so
practise on leather scraps until you are confident.

Tubular rivets consist of two cylindrical parts, the stem
and cap, and come in a variety of sizes and finishes such as
gilt, brass, antiqued brass, nickel and copper. Push the stem
through both layers of leather from the underside (the side
that will not be seen). Then press the cap onto the stem and

place it on the anvil. Place the setter over the cap and strike it with a hammer. This causes the stem to compress and expand, forming a tight seal within the cap.

Although the process is straightforward it is easy to damage the rivet. The most frequent mistakes made when riveting are: not using an anvil and setter, using the wrong size anvil and setter and using the wrong length of stem. Not using an anvil and setter will flatten and mark the domed head of the cap, as will a setter that does not fit the cap snugly. A stem that is too long will bend over and make a mess, and too short a stem will not seal correctly. A correctly fitting stem should protrude approximately $^1/_{16}$ in (1.5mm) above the surface of the leather when the two pieces are pressed tightly together.

Bifurcated rivets are single cylindrical shapes that are split in two for approximately three quarters of their length. Push the rivet through the leather from the topside, then place it on the anvil, which has a concave surface to prevent flattening of the head. Place the setter between the split and tap it to splay out the prongs, then tap directly onto the prongs until they are flush with the leather surface.

Press studs come in many different forms and consist of male and female parts which are fixed to the leather to form a simple fastening. As with tubular rivets each part is fixed with an anvil and setter, and it is important to use the correct ones for each part as a damaged stud will not perform correctly. They are useful for forming simple closures on purses or bag flaps. They can be used effectively on the ends of belts where the user may wish to switch buckles.

Eyelets can be used to join thinner leather but are more commonly used as reinforcement and are again fixed using an anvil and setter or purpose-made pliers.

Glues

Having a pot of leather glue in the workshop is very useful, but it is not a good idea to use glue to form a joint as most will become unstuck over time. However, sometimes it is useful to glue a joint together to hold it in place until a permanent fixing can be made. Take advice from your supplier as to which one to purchase, but always check the directions before use.

Stitching

Regardless of how well an item is cut and prepared, bad and untidy stitching will ruin the project. Care and patience should be exercised, concentrating on neatness rather than speed; this will come naturally with practice. Choice of needles, stitch length and threads all contribute in the appearance of the finished product.

The two methods of stitching used are hand stitching or machine stitching. Whilst sewing machines have the advantage of speed, for all but the thinnest of leathers an industrial sewing machine would be required and these can be expensive (even secondhand), plus they require space. One advantage that hand stitching has over machine stitching is its strength. Machines use a hook and loop method to pick up the thread (so that pulling at a loose thread could undo the entire row of stitching), while hand stitching crosses itself, so if a stitch is cut the rest remain in place.

As you become more practised you may develop techniques that differ from those given. There is nothing wrong with this, providing that the end result is the same and it is a safe method of working. Remember, this is supposed to be for enjoyment not an endurance test. If you find that you are getting frustrated, put the work down and come back to it later.

Basic Stitching Rules

1. Always stitch towards yourself except when finishing off.
2. Where practicable, always stitch with the jaws of the clams supporting the work.
3. Avoid using knots as they can be unsightly; better to go over the first stitch twice.
4. Always finish off by going back 2½ stitches. Items made of very heavy leather or where the stitching will come under a lot of strain will require more finishing stitches.
5. The thread must be well waxed to prevent it from shredding while in use. Waxing may need to be repeated on very long runs of stitching.
6. Concentrate on neatness. Speed will come with practice.
7. The stitching awl should be pushed through the leather in one clean movement and at right angles to the work piece; otherwise there is a possibility of the stitch breaking through into the previous one.
8. Resist the urge to wiggle the awl about or use it as a lever; this is one of the main causes of breaking awl blades.
9. Ensure that each stitch is pulled tight; loose stitching will be a weak point.
10. On straps that will come under strain (such as handbag straps and handles) avoid stitching across the grain as this weakens the leather.

11. On most pieces of work the main points of strain will be on the first and last stitches; always secure these with a double stitch or over stitch. (The last stitch will be re-enforced in the finishing-off process.)

Initial Preparation

The leather will require marking before stitching and, as these marks are permanent, always think before acting. Having spent a lot of time preparing your project you do not want to ruin it with a wrongly placed stitch mark. Assess the project. Is there going to be any great strain on the stitching? Do you want a fine decorative look or a more rustic look? What colour thread should be used? These factors will influence the choice of stitch length and threads.

CHOOSING STITCH LENGTH, THREAD AND NEEDLES

As a general rule the greater number of stitches per inch the neater the end result. However, stitching at anything above 8 stitches per inch (25mm) takes a considerable amount of care and practice as the distance between each stitch is less. Consideration must also be given to the strength of the join as the more stitches per inch the more holes are punched through the leather thus making it weaker.

Choice of thread weight will depend on the overall effect required, the stitch length and usage of the finished item. Heavier threads require larger needles so it would be impracticable to use an 18/6 thread on a stitch length of 12 per inch, and an 18/3 thread used with a stitch length of 6 per inch would be totally lost.

Many people find threading needles quite difficult, and the temptation for the beginner is to grab a larger needle. Resist the temptation and persevere; the smaller the needle, the smaller the hole required to allow the needle to pass through. If you used a stitch length of 10 per inch with an 18/5 thread and No.1 needle, the size of hole required for the needle to pass through would probably break into the previous stitch. Fine threads up to and including 18/4 will thread through No.4 needles and 18/5 and 18/6 threads will thread through a No.2 needle. Obviously larger threads and hand-made threads will require larger needles, but always use the smallest possible.

As a general rule of thumb the larger the stitch length, the heavier the thread used. Stitch lengths up to and includ-

Make a double stitch by starting on the second stitch mark (the one prior to the furthest one from you), going forward to the first then back to the second.

The over stitch starts on the first stitch mark. Equalize the threads, then cross them over, forming a loop over the edge of the leather. Pass the needles through the stitch hole in turn and tighten. This stitch is ideal for pulling the leather together behind the buckle bar, but the method that you use will depend on the project and personal judgement.

To create an over stitch, bring the needles through the first stitch mark, cross the threads over and pass the needles back through the hole.

ing 6 stitches per inch (25mm) use an 18/5 or 18/6 thread or heavier. Stitch lengths of 7 or 8 per inch use an 18/4 thread. For stitch lengths of 10 per inch and above use an 18/3 or finer thread.

STITCH MARKING

There are many factors that will influence the distance of the stitch marks from the edge of the leather (such as weight of thread, length of stitch, the overall aesthetic look of the project). Each project within this book will give guidelines for the stitch marking, and with a little experience judging these distances will become second nature.

For practice purposes, draw a line $1/8$ in (3mm) from the edge of the leather using a screw crease, dividers or groover. Place the stitch marker upright at one end of the leather with

Fraying the end of the thread, then waxing and twisting it between the fingers produces a tapered end which aids the threading of needles.

To wax the thread, use the thumb to hold the thread against the wax while pulling with the free hand.

the top of the stitches just under the line and strike it with a mallet. If a groove line was used, mark directly into the groove. Reposition the stitch marker overlapping the last previously-made stitch mark and strike again with the mallet. Continue in this manner until the intended length of stitch marking has been completed. Alternatively a pricking wheel may be used (for use of stitch markers and pricking wheels, *see* Chapter 1).

PREPARING THE THREAD

There are two methods of preparing the thread for threading through the needles, but for both methods start by cutting a length of thread approximately three times the length of the stitch markings. If a long seam is to be stitched it is better to finish partway along and cut a new thread than to have a thread so long that it gets tangled on everything in sight.

Method 1

Lay the end of the thread on the cutting mat and place the blade of a knife at an angle of 45 degrees away from you and approximately ¾in (19mm) in from the end of the thread. Pull the thread towards you applying slight pressure; this will un-ravel the thread and remove a few fibres. Keep working until the thread has a silk-like quality, then work a couple of strokes at the tip of the thread which will form a taper.

Wax the thread well by holding it on the beeswax with your thumb and pulling it towards you, ensuring the ends are well covered. If done correctly the ends should have a fine taper making them easier to thread.

Method 2

Wax the thread as in Method 1, then flatten the end between the thumb and forefinger or by placing it on the bench and rubbing it with the back of an awl handle. Using a sharp pair of scissors cut the end at an angle to form a taper.

LOCKING THE NEEDLES

The needles can be 'locked' to prevent them from becoming unthreaded. Pull 3in (76mm) of thread through the eye, lay it alongside the main thread and stab through the centre of both with the needle; repeat this process approximately ½in (12mm) below the first stab, pull the needle through the thread and smooth it with your fingers, applying more wax if required. This process is not essential as the wax on the thread tends to keep it in place; it is a matter of personal choice.

LEFT:
Locking the needles: Split the thread with the needle and pull the thread over the eye of the needle.

BELOW:
With the clams resting against the left thigh, use the stirrup to exert pressure on the jaws.

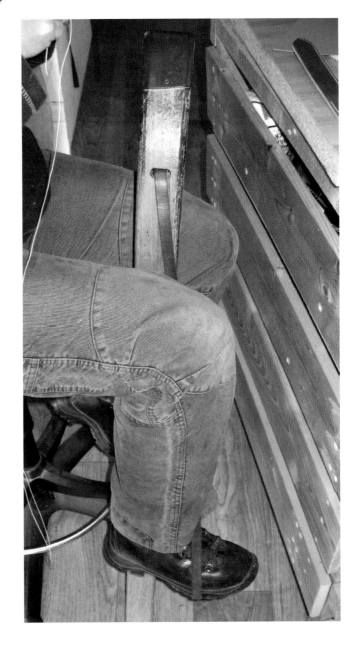

PREPARING TO STITCH

Sit comfortably with the clams between your knees resting against your left thigh and foot in the stirrup (if used). Using your right hand, place your thumb against the left jaws of the clams and the remaining fingers on the right; apply equal pressure to both jaws, which will open the clams.

For many this proves quite a difficult task, and initially the tension screw may need to be slackened (*see* Chapter 1: Tools). Beginners often try to open the clams while they are being held closed via the stirrup, but unless you have amazingly strong fingers they cannot exert as much pressure as your leg, so make sure that you release any pressure from the stirrup. This method of opening the clams is not cast in stone, and many develop their own technique.

Place the work in the clams; the jaws should be close to the stitch marks, leaving enough room for the awl to run through and supporting the work area. Start at the furthest stitch mark from you and work towards yourself. As the stitching reaches the end of the clam jaws, release the pressure on the jaws and slide the work forward.

When working with light coloured threads and leathers cover the jaws of the clams with white paper to prevent the accumulated debris on the clam jaws being transferred to the work piece.

Before starting to stitch make sure that all the required tools are within reach (i.e. stitching awl, thread, wax, scissors, small pliers, clickers knife or equivalent).

When cutting off the excess thread at the end of the stitching run, where possible use a knife rather than scissors as this

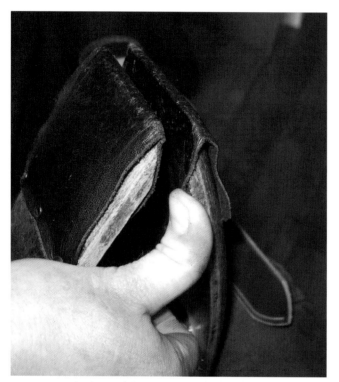

Open the jaws of the clams with fingers and thumb.

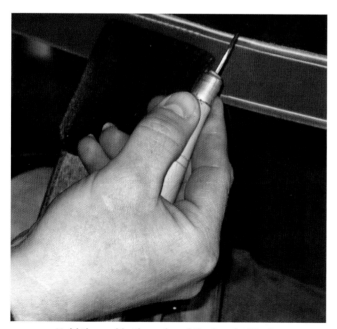

Hold the awl in the palm of the hand with the thumb in the notch.

allows you to get much closer to the leather – but be careful not to cut through any of the existing stitches.

Until you are confident of your ability, start by practising on a single thickness of leather, then practise on a double thickness. Don't be tempted to skip this stage as stitching two pieces of leather together is very different from stitching through one.

Take the stitching awl in the right hand and position it so that the heel of the handle is against your palm and with your thumb in the notch. When stitching try to keep the needles and awl in your hands at all times and try not to look at the back of the work. This may prove awkward initially but persevere as it will lead to neater faster stitching.

It can sometimes be difficult to push the needle through the stitch holes, especially when finishing off. If this happens use the handle of the awl to push the needle in as far as possible then grasp it with the pliers and pull it through.

Types of Stitches

SADDLE STITCH

This stitch is probably the most widely used, and if done properly it should look the same as a machine stitch. It is also the trickiest to master, but once mastered, all the other stitch types will be straightforward.

Prepare a length of thread with a needle threaded onto each end. Then place the work into the clams as described above.

(*Note*: It is easier to describe this technique as a continuous sequence, but for reasons already discussed remember that the first stitch should be secured.)

1. Initially leave the needles and thread on the bench. Take up the awl as described and locate the first stitch mark (the one furthest from you). With the awl blade in line with the angle of the stitch mark, use the palm of your hand to push it through the leather. It is important to keep the awl at right angles to the leather surface; any deviation from this and you may break into the adjoining stitch. It sometimes helps to support the back of the area of leather being stitched with the thumb of your left hand, but be careful to keep it clear of the awl coming through.

2. Reposition the awl so that it is held in the crook of the thumb and first finger. Then with the same hand pick up

one of the needles using the thumb and first finger. Push the needle through the hole from right to left, then pull it through with the left hand. Pick up the remaining needle in the right hand as before and level the needles; equal threads on both sides of the work allows uniform tension to be applied to each stitch.

3. Here comes the tricky bit. Using only the right hand, switch the needle to between the first two fingers, holding the eye against the awl handle with the middle (second) finger. Return the awl to its stitching position. Locate the next stitch mark, line up the awl blade and push it through.

4. We now come to the needle in the left hand. Place the first finger on top of the needle then place it on the awl blade. Withdraw the awl slowly and at the same follow the blade through the hole with the needle. Try to do this without looking at the back side of the work; after a while you will develop a sixth sense for locating the awl.

5. Reposition the tools in the right hand so that the awl is resting in the crook of the thumb and the needle between the thumb and first finger. Cross the needle with the needle coming through the leather and firmly grasp both needles between the thumb and first finger and pull the needles through.

6. As the needle clears the hole turn your wrist towards the leather and place the right hand needle on top of the thread in the stitch hole, push it through, then grasp it with the left hand and pull it clear of the hole. (Be careful not to split the thread. Pulling the left thread back as the right needle passes through will help to prevent this happening).

7. Keeping the needles and awl in your hands, pull the threads up tight with equal tension on both.

8. Congratulations, you have just completed your first stitch. Repeat the sequence from Step 3 until you have reached the end of the work.

9. At the end of the stitching run you will need to 'lock off' the last stitches. This is done by going back 2½ stitches. Do not use the stitching awl to open the holes as the sharp point may cut the existing stitches. If necessary use one of the needles as the awl. Having gone back two full stitches, pass the needle on the good side of the work (right side) through the next stitch hole in the sequence to the back. This forms the half stitch and leaves both threads on the back of the work (left side).

10. Finally, use a sharp knife to cut the threads as close to the work as possible, taking care not to cut any of the existing stitches. (A knife allows you to get closer to the work than scissors.)

SADDLE STITCH

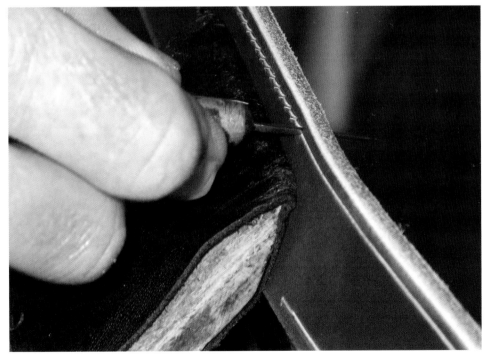

Line up the blade with the first stitch mark and push it through.

SADDLE STITCH *continued*

Pull the threads through and equalize them.

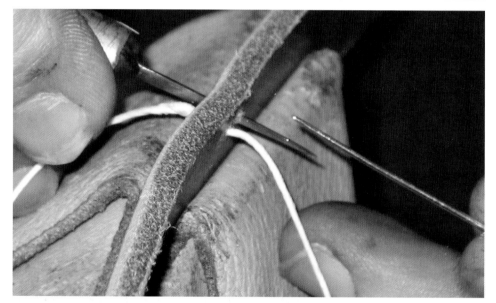

Push the awl through the next stitch mark; place needle on the awl blade and as the awl blade is retracted, follow through with the needle.

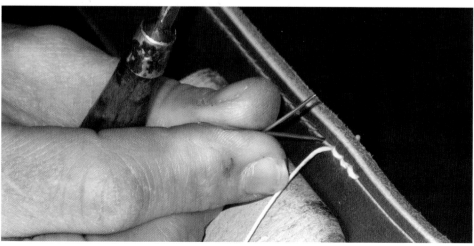

Grasp the needle between the thumb and forefinger, making a cross with the needle in the right hand.

As the needle clears the hole, turn the wrist and place the right hand needle into the hole.

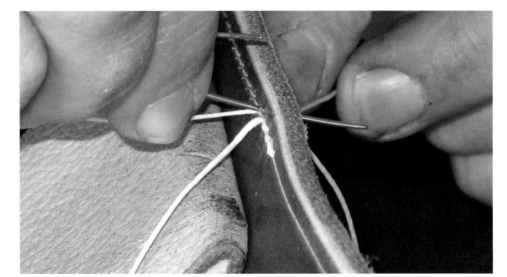

Pull the threads up tight.

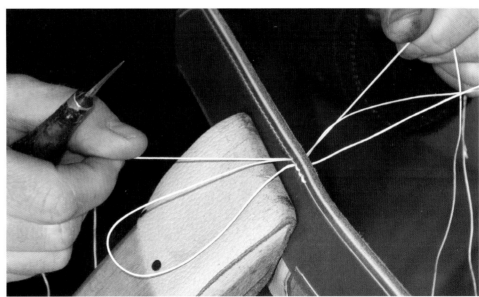

To finish, go over the last stitches, ending up on the back of the work.

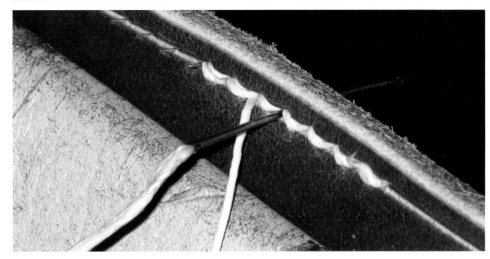

CROSSING OVER

When stitching two parallel lines of stitching, such as buckle returns, it is quicker and sometimes safer if they are stitched with one continuous thread. To do this, once the first side of stitching is complete, the threads need to be crossed to the other side. The technique we are going to use is known as a hidden twist, which not only looks neater but also protects the thread from wear.

This technique can also be used with the back stitch.

1. Keeping the line of the existing stitches, form a stitch that goes over the end of the top piece of leather.
2. Take the needle on the front of the work, go back one stitch mark and push the needle through the existing hole so that it comes out between the two pieces of leather.

Pull the thread through, then repeat the process with the needle on the back.

3. Pull both threads tight, then pierce the corresponding stitch mark on the opposite side. (Be careful not to cut the threads). Pass the needles through these stitch holes from between the two pieces of leather to the outside of the work. (One should come to the front and the other to the back; it does not matter which one goes where.)
4. Repeat Step 1, then continue the stitching sequence. If done correctly, there should be a double stitch going over the end of the top piece of leather and the crossed thread should be hidden between the two pieces of leather.

CROSSING OVER WHEN STITCHING RETURNS

The last stitch should go over the end of the return.

Come back one stitch, angling the needle so that it comes out between the two pieces of leather.

Bring the needles to the opposite side and bring the needles from between the leather to the outside.

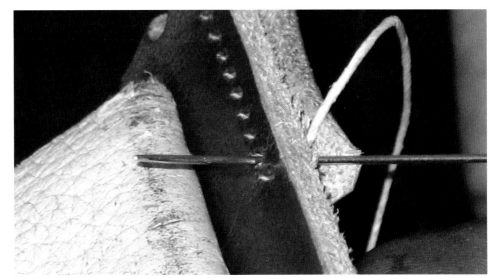

Go back over the end of the return.

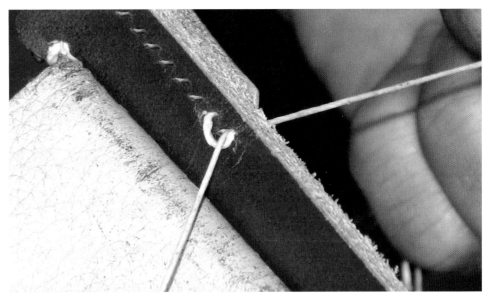

Continue stitching as normal.

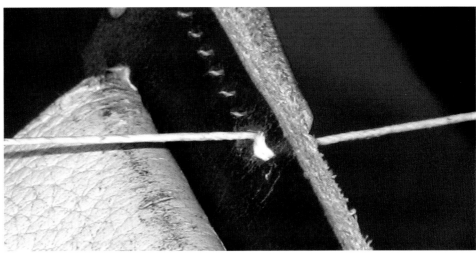

BACK STITCH

This stitch is done with a single needle and thread and can be used where the back of the work is hidden. Wax a length of thread and thread a needle onto one end. One line of thought is to place a knot in the opposite end. As the knot needs to be fairly large to prevent it from pulling through the stitch hole, it can look unsightly if it is not hidden away. It is often better to 'lock' the first stitch which is the method described here.

1. The starting point for this type of stitch is one stitch mark in from the first. This is because the sequence for the back stitch is forward one then back two. With the awl in your right hand and the needle in the left, line up the awl with the stitch mark and push it through the leather.
2. Using the same technique for lining up the needle with the awl described in the saddle stitch, pull the needle and thread through the hole leaving approximately 2in (50mm) on the back of the work.
3. Move forward to the first stitch mark, pierce it with the awl and pull the needle through to the back. The thread on the front of the work should hang loosely forming a loop.
4. Bring the needle back through the first stitch hole made, taking care not to split the thread. Grasp the trailing thread in the left hand and pull the stitch tight. Repeat Step 3. (When pulled tight the first stitch will be a double stitch.)
5. Move back two stitch marks (you should now be on the third stitch mark), pierce it with the awl and bring the thread to the front, pulling it tight. Move forward one and pull the needle through, leaving the thread on the front of the work hanging loosely. When pulling up the first two or three stitches weave the trailing thread into the back of them to secure it; then cut it off.
6. Move back two stitch marks, pull the thread tight, then move forward one and pull the needle through to the back. Continue in this manner until the whole stitching run is complete. To finish off go over the last and second to last stitches twice.

BACK STITCH

Start one stitch back.

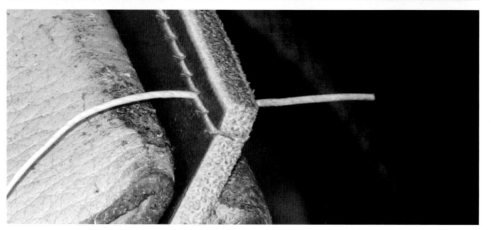

Bring the needle from the back of the work leaving a 'tail' of thread.

Go forward one stitch and pass the needle to the back of the work. Repeat the first stitch to make it a double stitch.

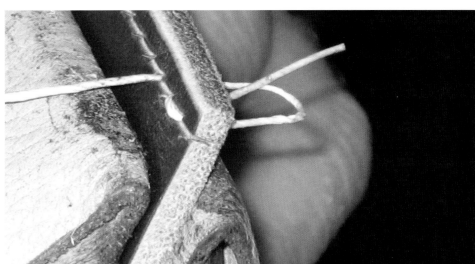

Come forward to the next stitch mark in sequence (third stitch mark back).

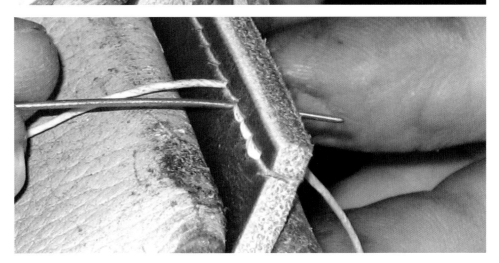

Pass the needle through the previous stitch hole to fill the gap; continue in this manner, forward then back, to the end of the stitch run.

Go over the penultimate and last
stitches twice.

RUNNING STITCH

This is a simple stitch where the needle is passed in and out
down the length of the stitching run. Start from the back side
of the work making the first stitch a double stitch to avoid the
use of a knot.

A variation on this stitch is when the end of the stitch run
is reached, go back along it filling in the gaps. This can sometimes be useful when repairing the seams of bags that cannot
be held in the clams as you need one hand free to hold the
seam together. However, it is difficult to get a neat finish with
this stitch so do not use it on new work.

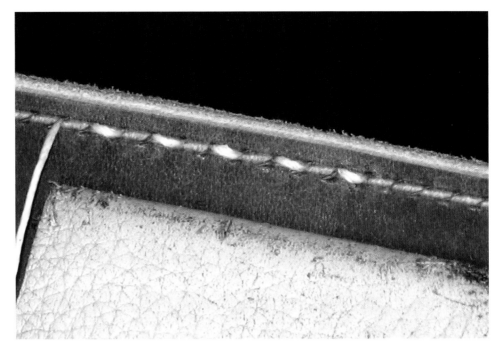

Simple running stitch.

At the end of the stitch run, the gaps can be filled by stitching back along the stitch line.

FINISHING

Where possible it is always a good idea to place the work on a flat surface and tap the stitching with a hammer to flatten it. This helps to reduce the wear on the stitches. Like the jaws of the clams, the face of the hammer can accumulate debris that can be transferred to the leather, so always check the work surface and hammer face, cleaning them if necessary. When working with light coloured threads or leather place the work piece between two pieces of clean paper before you start.

Lacing (Thonging)

Lacing, or thonging, is stitching done with a thin piece of leather rather than thread. It can be looked upon as a more decorative form of stitching and can be used when making handbags, moccasins or any item that would benefit from an attractive finish. It is not suited to items that will come under a lot of strain, however.

Some leatherwork books will describe this process as thronging, while others describe it as lacing. How you refer to it depends on which name you heard first and really does not matter. There may be some miniscule difference between lacing and thronging, but for the purposes of this book we will take both terms as meaning the same.

Although it is possible to make your own lacing it is a fiddly and time consuming process, so you will probably want to buy it readymade. Lacing comes in many finishes and colours and can be flat, round or square, with flat lacing being the most commonly used. It may be purchased in single lengths or on a continuous roll. A lot of lacing is used when doing the fancier stitches; single lengths would only suffice for small projects, so it is better to buy a roll.

ADDITIONAL TOOLS

- **Lacing needle** (*see* Chapter 1).
- **Lacing fid** This is used to enlarge the holes before inserting the lacing needle. Whilst this is a useful tool, if you are doing a lot of lacing, a large awl with the edges and point rounded (blunted) will suffice.
- **Lacing (thonging) chisels** These are similar to stitch markers. They have teeth set at regular intervals which cut in a horizontal plane or are angled. Like the stitch marker they are placed on the leather at 90 degrees to its surface, then struck with a mallet. Unlike stitch markers they are punched right through the leather. The number of teeth varies between 1 and 8, with the single tooth chisel being used to go around corners.
- **Lacing pony** These are similar to stitching clams, but they are self supporting and the jaws are made to open wider. The jaws are not sprung, and the tension is manually adjusted. The purchase of this equipment is not necessary as the stitching clams will normally suffice.

PREPARATION

To allow the lace to pass through the leather it will require punching with either a hole punch or lacing chisel. Punch both pieces of leather to be joined. It is extremely important that they are a mirror image of each other or they will not line up when laced. If possible, to achieve a mirror image punch the two pieces of leather together using clamps to prevent them from moving. If this is not possible, the second piece will need to be marked and punched exactly the same as the first.

It is easier to work around corners that have been rounded or that have the sharp right angle nicked off at 45 degrees. As with stitching, make sure that all the tools that you will require are to hand before starting, and if possible it is better to hold the work in the clams.

Start by using the dividers, screw crease or groover to mark a line $\frac{1}{8}$in (3mm) from the edge of the leather around the area to be laced.

If you are using a lacing chisel place the work onto the lead block or punching surface. Using the single pronged chisel mark the corners (these marks should follow the angle of the corner) by holding the chisel at 90 degrees to the leather surface and striking it with a mallet, remembering that these chisels are punched right through the leather.

Working out from the corners, take the multi-pronged chisel and work around the area to be laced, lining up the last chisel mark made with the first of the next to be punched.

As you approach a corner you may find that the last mark leaves an uneven gap. We overcome this problem by punching the last sequence using the single pronged punch estimating an even gap between each mark. A single uneven gap will stand out like a sore thumb whereas a series of slightly differing gaps will blend in.

If you are punching holes set your dividers to a suitable gap – ¼in (6mm) is a good distance to practice with – and working out from the corners, walk the dividers along the line. (A stitch marker of an appropriate size may also be used). It is a good idea to check the distances between the corners before starting and set the dividers so that they leave an even gap without having to adjust them as you reach the next corner.

Punch out the holes using either a revolving punch or single punch. The size of hole will depend on the width of lacing that is being used, but always use the smallest hole size possible. For most types of flat lacing a No.1 hole punch should be sufficient.

If there are no right-angled corners on the stitch line (i.e. all corners are rounded), there is no need to work out from the corners. Start at the beginning of the stitch line and work

Lace in lacing needle: gently press the jaws together with pliers.

around to the end. However as the end is reached the gaps are still adjusted (if necessary) as described. This applies whether using a lacing chisel or hole punch.

THREADING THE NEEDLE

Make sure that the end of the lace is cut square, and skive about ¼in (6mm) off the flesh side to approximately half its thickness. Nick off both corners at 45 degrees. (This is to prevent them snagging as the needle is pulled through the holes). Open the end of the needle taking care not to bend the ends and negate the spring action. Place the lace between the jaws so that the prongs will pierce the grain side; allow the jaws to close, then gently press the together using pliers if necessary. Gently tug on the lace to make sure that it is secure.

RUNNING, BUCK AND WHIP STITCH

These three lacing stitches are suitable for use on thinner leathers and are all fairly self explanatory with the exception of starting and finishing.

The running stitch is performed in the same manner as the running stitch described in the hand-stitching section. On the front of the work the grain side of the lace will be showing and on the back the flesh side. The best results are achieved using an angled chisel or by punching holes.

The buck stitch is the same as the running stitch, except that the grain side of the lace is showing on both the front and back of the work and the stitches take on a diamond appearance. This effect is achieved in two ways. First, the leather must be punched with a flat chisel as opposed to an angled

TWISTED LACING

Due to the long lengths of lacing used it is very easy to get the lace twisted. Before pushing the needle through the hole run your thumb and forefinger along the entire length of the lace to remove any twist, and ensure that the needle is inserted with the grain side of the lace in the correct position.

Having pulled it through if you find that the lace is twisted, gently twisting the lace in the opposite direction of the twist, pull it back and forth through the stitch hole until the twist is worked out.

chisel or hole punch. Second, before the needle is inserted into the stitch hole it is twisted so that the grain side of the lace is uppermost.

The whip stitch is yet another basic stitch that goes over the edges of the leather rather than laying flat on the surface. A variation on this stitch is having reached the end of the stitch run, work back to the start point. The lacing will form a cross over the edge.

Starting

1. Take the unthreaded end of the lace and place a small slit through the centre running parallel to its length approximately ¼in (6mm) from the end.

RUNNING, BUCK AND WHIP STITCHES

Slit the end of the lace and pierce to secure.

Angle the needle up between the two
pieces of leather.

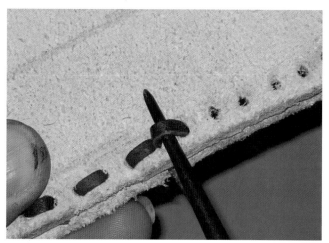

Pulling up loose stitches before trimming lace.

2. Part the two pieces of leather. Push the needle through the first stitch hole in the back piece only and pull the lace through, leaving approximately ½in (12mm) showing.

3. *For running and buck stitch* pass the needle through the next stitch hole in sequence, through the slit in the tab and out of the front of the work. Pull the lace through and tighten the stitch.

4. *For whip stitch* pass the needle through the next hole in sequence on the front of the work (this will be the second stitch hole in) through the slit in the tab and out of the back. Pull the lace through and tighten the stitch. If this has been done correctly the lace should be laying across the top of the joined edges.

Finishing

1. *For running and buck stitch* come through the last stitch hole as normal, leaving the penultimate stitch slightly loose. Come forward one stitch hole (this hole will already have a lace running through it), push the needle through the hole at angle so that it comes up between the two pieces of leather.

2. *For whip stitch* leave the penultimate stitch slightly loose and angle the needle so that it comes up between the two pieces of leather and behind the penultimate stitch.

3. Use a stylus or pointed awl to tighten the stitches, then trim off the excess.

DOUBLE AND TRIPLE LOOP STITCHES

These types of lacing stitches will completely cover the joined edges and on inspection they look very similar; the difference is in the resulting thickness of the lace pattern. There is also a single loop stitch, but the differences between it and the double loop stitch are minute, and personally I have never found an occasion to use it. For these reasons it has been omitted from this book.

When practising these stitches try to get the pattern to slant slightly towards the good side of the work rather than sitting on top of the joined edges. For some reason this seems to give the work a more professional finish.

To achieve a neat finish it is important that the grain side of the lace is uppermost and that even tension is applied to each stitch throughout the resulting pattern.

For both these types of stitches, the needle is always passed through the leather or the crosses from the front of the work.

DOUBLE LOOP STITCH

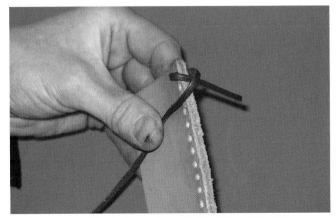

Start on the first hole leaving a 'tail' of about 2in (50mm).

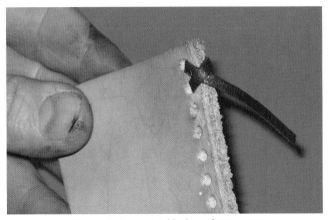

Go through the second hole to form a cross.

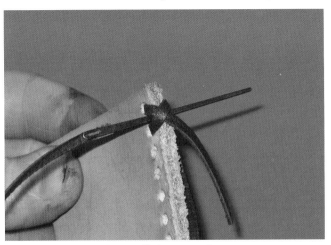

Pass the needle between the cross.

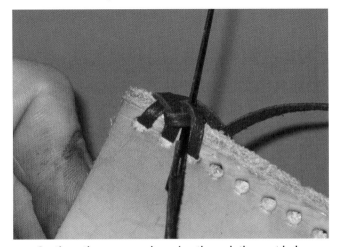

Continue the sequence by going through the next hole, then through the cross.

When going around corners, go through the three corner holes twice to maintain the pattern.

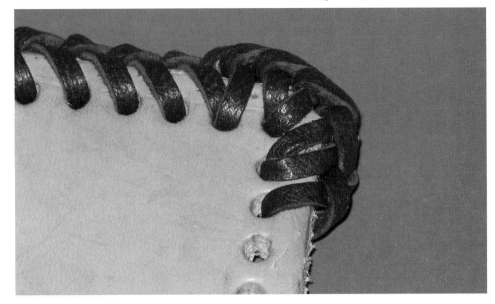

TRIPLE LOOP STITCH

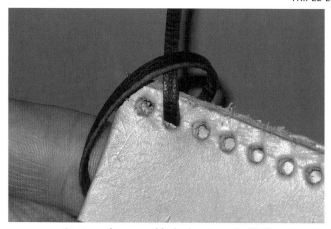

Start on the second hole, leaving a 'tail' of about 2in (50mm).

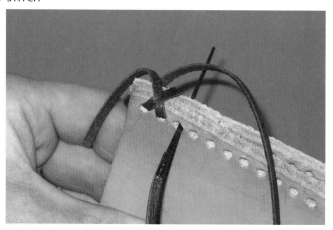

Pass the needle through the first hole, then through the third.

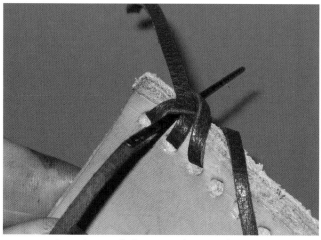

Pass the needle between the cross formed between holes 1 and 2.

Continue the sequence along the stitch run.

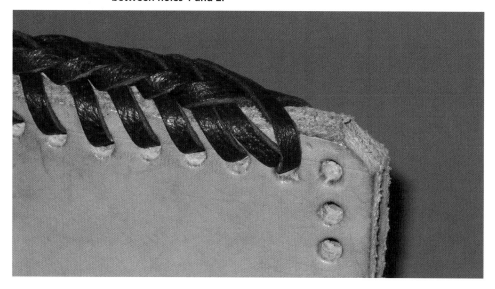

Finishing double and triple loop stitches: Pass the needle through the last stitch hole, angling it up between the two pieces of leather.

Double Loop

1. Pull the lace through the first stitch hole from the front of the work, leaving a tab of about 1in (25mm).
2. Fold the tab over the edge of the leather, bring the lace to the front of the work, push the needle through the second stitch hole and pull the lace through to the back of the work and tighten the stitch. The lace should now have formed a cross with the tab caught under it.
3. Working from the front, pass the needle between the resultant cross. Tighten the stitch, then pass the needle through the next stitch hole. Continue this sequence along the stitch run.
4. To maintain the pattern around the corners you will need to go through the three corner holes twice.

Triple Loop

1. Starting on the second stitch hole and working from the front of the work, pull the lace through, leaving a tab of about 1in (25mm). Pass the needle through the first hole to form the cross of lacing, then go through the third stitch hole.
2. Pass the needle between the initial cross, then through the next stitch hole. Continue along the length of the stitch run, moving forward to the next stitch hole, then passing through the cross on the hole before. Corners are tackled in the same manner as the double loop stitch.

Finishing

For both the double and triple loop stitches the method of finishing is the same. Complete the last stitch as normal. Come over back through the last hole (already occupied with lacing) but when coming through this stitch hole, angle the needle so that it comes out between the two pieces of leather and the last stitch. Tighten the stitch and trim off the excess.

Joining Laces

For the double and triple loop stitches the ratio between the amount of lacing required to the length of stitch run is roughly 8 to 1. This can present a problem as any more than about 5–6ft (1.5–1.9 m) of lacing can become unmanageable, especially for beginners. Also the constant pulling through the stitch holes can cause the latter parts to fray; this tends to be more of a problem when lacing chisels are used. Taking this into account, at some point you will need to join the lacing.

JOINING LACES

Pierce the new lace and trim the old lace leaving about 1in (25mm).

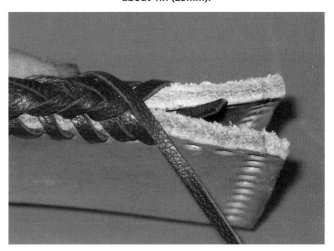

Continue the sequence with the new lace, locking the tail of the old lace between the two pieces of leather.

This process is the same for any of the stitch types described.

1. Slit the end of the new lace as you would when starting the running, buck or whip stitch.
2. Place the new lace between the two pieces of leather, lining up the slit with the next stitch hole in the sequence. When this stitch is made, pierce the slit in the new lace and bring the needle up between the two pieces of leather. Cut the old lace leaving approximately 1in (25mm). Continue the sequence using the new lace. The tail of the old lace should be lying between the stitches and the joined edges of the leather.

The vast array of dyes available.

Colouring Leather

Dyeing

Dyes are generally used to colour natural vegetable tanned leather, but even if you are using dyed leather the flesh coloured edges will require dyeing.

There is a vast array of different coloured dyes on the market which will allow you to give vent to your artistic tendencies. The main types of dyes are spirit, alcohol or water based which all soak into the surface of the leather. In fact there is not much that they will not soak into, so always protect your work surfaces and clothes and wear gloves. (It is worth noting that many countries are phasing out the use of solvent-based dyes.)

Dyes are purchased ready mixed or in powder form, although finding spirit dyes in a powder form is becoming increasingly difficult. If you get the powdered form you will need to equip yourself with airtight containers to mix and store them in. As spirit dyes are mixed with surgical or methylated spirits, and water dyes with warm water, beware of which one you have purchased. Powder dyes can be diluted or strengthened to alter the colour shade. Dyes of the same type can be mixed to produce different colours and shades. (Do not mix water based and spirit based dyes.)

Dyes should be applied after any carving and stamping has been performed and before the project is assembled.

APPLYING DYE

The colour of the leather can dramatically affect the final colour of the dye, so always test it on a piece of scrap that has come from the same hide as the project in hand.

Firstly dampen the surface of the leather with water (a bottle with a spray nozzle is ideal). This allows the dye to penetrate more evenly. Working from the corner of the leather, apply the dye in small circular motions using a sponge, soft cloth or cotton wool ball. Better results are achieved by applying several layers, but be aware that the more layers applied, the deeper the colour will be. Dyes dry fairly quickly, especially the first layer, so you will have to work quickly but methodically. Additional layers should be applied while the dye is still wet.

Antique Finish

Antique finish does not dye the leather in the strictest sense, but it tones down the existing colour and brings out the grain in the leather. The colours available tend to be shades of brown or tan. It can be used on its own or over a previously dyed surface, but always test it first as the original colour may be altered. While it is not essential to use these finishes they are ideal on curved or stamped leather to emphasize the relief.

The finish comes in two forms, antique finish and antique stain. Antique finish is thick and creamy and has a wax content that can be buffed to a shine, while antique stain is in a liquid form.

APPLYING FINISHES

Apply both finishes in the same manner as you would a dye, building up the layers to achieve the desired effect. When complete buff up with a soft cloth. Antique stain is the easier of the two to apply, but you do not get as rich a finish as with antique finish.

When using antique finish have a kitchen roll to hand to remove the excess. The best results are achieved by rubbing lightly, building up a thick layer, then removing it while it is still wet; if allowed to dry it will look really dark and streaky. If it does dry before you can remove it, go over the area with more of the finish to loosen it up, then wipe off immediately.

Edge Dyeing

Any project will benefit from having the raw edges of the leather dyed. Where two pieces of leather are joined, edge dyeing done properly will cement the two together giving the appearance of one thickness. Edge dyes are specially formulated for the purpose; ordinary dyes dry out too quickly leaving it difficult to polish up the edges. Woollen daubers are best used for application; they are cheap and readily available from leather craft stockists.

Mixing wall paper size or paste (available at any good hardware or DIY store) with powder edge dye aids the sealing properties and helps to give a good shine. Use a 10½oz (300g) coffee jar and mix 5tsp (25ml) dye with 2tsp (10ml) wallpaper size. Fill the jar with hot (not boiling) water and stir until all lumps have been dissolved. Adding more powder or diluting the mixture will strengthen or weaken the solution respectively.

APPLYING EDGE FINISHES

Slickers, polishing bones, burnishing wheels can all be purchased for polishing the edges, but anything with a smooth

---

CLEANING LEATHER BEFORE DYEING

During the process of working the leather, grease marks and dirt can accumulate on the surface, which can resist the absorption of the dye. It is a matter of judgement on whether the surface is cleaned before dyeing, but once the dye is applied there is no going back. A blotchy dyed finish could ruin your project, so advice to beginners would be to always clean before dyeing.

OXALIC ACID

There are ready-made cleaners available (use these in accordance with the manufacturer's instructions), but I have achieved better results using oxalic acid, which comes in a crystallized form and can be purchased at most chemists.

Mix 1tsp (5ml) oxalic acid to ¼pt (120ml) warm water, stirring until all the crystals have dissolved. Using a soft cloth or sponge rub the surface of the leather using small circular movements. Use a clean sponge or cloth and immediately wash the surface with clean water and leave to dry.

SAFETY PRECAUTIONS

Although oxalic acid is classified as a weak acid, it is still an acid and it is poisonous. It is not suitable for use by children. Always wear gloves when handling and store it away immediately after use, out of reach of children and in containers that are clearly labelled.

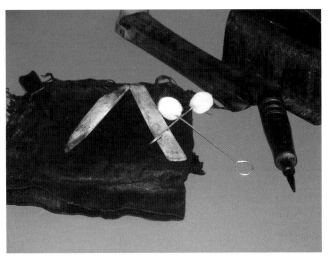

An array of edge dying implements: polishing bones, slickers and daubers.

Applying edge dye using a dauber.

To remove and polish the edges, grasp the strap on both edges and pull the strap quickly through the cloth.

Dye can be applied to groove lines with a pipe cleaner.

After application, polish the groove line using a pointed bone.

hard surface will suffice. An effective method is to wrap a cloth around a scrap piece of leather – do not wash the cloth as the dirtier it becomes the better it works.

Carry out any necessary edge shaving before applying the dye. Taking care not to allow the dye to bleed into the leather surface, apply the dye to the edges; then briskly rub with your chosen polishing implement until a smooth shine finish is achieved. The dye must be removed while still wet. On larger areas or in hot weather it may be necessary to do a little at a time.

A quick method of polishing the edges on straps is to use the cloth wrapped around the leather. Dye both edges. Then wrap the cloth around the strap, holding it tight against the edges, and pull the strap quickly through your hand. The fibres lie better when the strap is pulled in the direction of the grain. The correct direction is recognized by feel. Pulling against the grain produces resistance against the cloth and gives a rough feeling whereas the strap will glide smoothly through the hand when pulled with the grain. Repeat this process to achieve the finish.

Groove lines made on pre-dyed leathers generally look better if they are also dyed. Use a pipe cleaner to apply the dye; then run a pointed bone along the line.

If the project is of natural vegetable tanned leather that is not going to be dyed it is still good practice to seal the edges with a neutral coloured sealer which is applied and polished in the same manner. Put 1tsp (5ml) of wallpaper size into a container and while stirring add hot water until the mixture has a watery paste-like texture. Keep a separate set of polishing materials for use on neutral sealers to avoid the transfer of dye. (If the project is to be dyed, dampen the edges with water, then polish; the use of sealers in this circumstance would prevent the dye from penetrating.)

Other Colouring Methods

Leather paints (normally acrylic) are not absorbed by the leather; they merely form a surface film. Nevertheless, after two or three coats they will cover even the darkest leather and are fairly flexible. They can be used to paint designs directly onto the surface or to colour the relief on stamps or carvings. Painted surfaces do not normally require any further finishing and should be applied after any dyeing; the dyed surface must be absolutely dry. Certain leather finishes can react with the paints causing them to run, so test on a piece of scrap leather.

Felt tip markers are another means of colouring leather. Use spirit based markers as water based markers can smudge when finishes are applied. Always try the markers on scrap pieces before using them on your project, as different makes and the varying properties of leather will affect the colour.

Finishing

Once a project is completed it is good practice to feed it with a good quality leather feed. This will not only remove the work marks such as finger prints, it feeds the leather and seals the surface preventing it from drying out. (Regular feeding is required to keep leather in good condition.) This is especially true on natural leathers that have been dyed as the feed will help to protect water based dyes from running.

Moulding

When vegetable tanned leather is soaked the fibres loosen, making it soft and pliable, which allows it to be embossed or moulded into shapes and to retain the shape when dry. The

CORRECTING CUTTING IMPERFECTIONS

While the accurate cutting of leather is of paramount importance there will be occasions when you wander off line, leaving the edges uneven. This is especially true when cutting shapes (circles are notoriously difficult). Don't panic. Leather, to a point, can be treated like wood. Uneven edges can be sanded using a sanding block or a piece of sandpaper wrapped around a block of wood held at 90 degrees to the leather edge.

Be positive and use a reasonable amount of pressure, but take care not to round the edge or slip and scratch the grain. The coarser the grade of sandpaper employed the quicker the sanding process, but with a coarser grade the fibres will be 'fluffed up' more than if a finer grade is used. For smaller imperfections use a fine grade, but if a coarse grade is used finish with a fine grade.

A surf form can also be used for this purpose and will remove the leather quicker than sandpaper. However, the disruption to the leather fibres is quite pronounced, so always finish with fine grade sandpaper.

technique has been used for centuries to produce items such as drinking vessels and helmets.

The complexity of the shape and the consistency of the leather being used will dictate how much soaking the leather will require. In many cases just dampening the leather is sufficient. Shapes can be moulded by hand or with the use of moulds.

This technique can be used with dyed vegetable tanned leathers (in our workshop we use it to make crupper loops for horse driving harnesses) but more care is needed, as bleaching and/or cracking the dyed grain surface is easily done. Beginners are better using natural leathers and dyeing it if required.

PRACTICE PROJECT

Belt Pouch

The purpose of this project is to consolidate many of the techniques discussed in this chapter (*see* Chapter 1 for guidance regarding the use of tools).

The leather used is natural vegetable tanned with a substance of $^3/_{32}$–$^1/_8$ in (2.5–3mm): 6–8oz. Other ma-

terials used in this example are stitching implements, lacing and a press stud; however, the lacing can be substituted with stitching. The stitching is marked at 7 per inch (25mm) and stitched with an 18/5 thread.

Belt pouch dimensions.

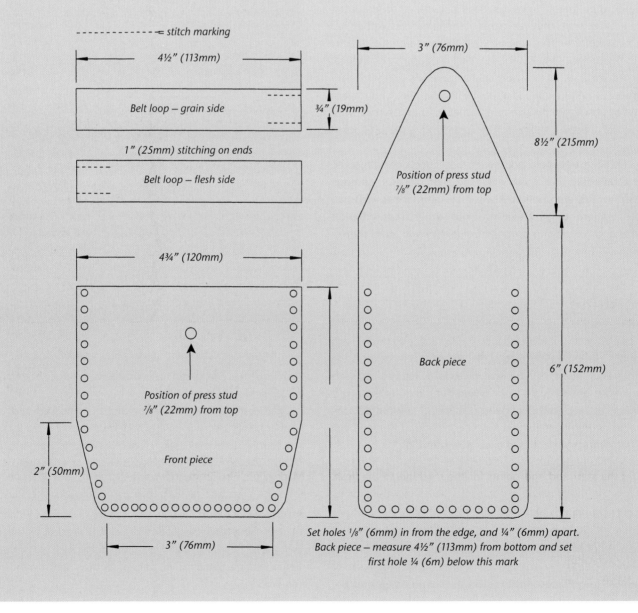

- - - - - - - - - - - - - - = *stitch marking*

4½" (113mm)

Belt loop – grain side   ¾" (19mm)

1" (25mm) stitching on ends

Belt loop – flesh side

4¾" (120mm)

Position of press stud $^7/_8$" (22mm) from top

2" (50mm)

Front piece

3" (76mm)

3" (76mm)

8½" (215mm)

Position of press stud $^7/_8$" (22mm) from top

Back piece

6" (152mm)

Set holes ⅛" (6mm) in from the edge, and ¼" (6mm) apart.
Back piece – measure 4½" (113mm) from bottom and set first hole ¼ (6m) below this mark

PRACTICE PROJECT: Belt Pouch *continued*

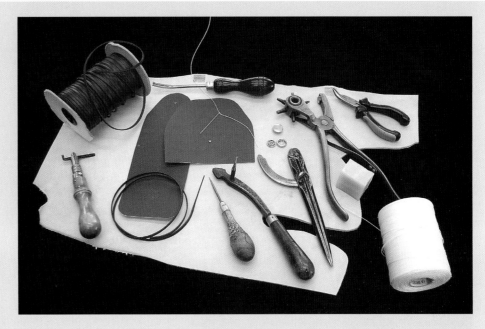

Required materials and tools.

STEP 1: CUTTING OUT

Transfer the given sizes onto a piece of stiff card and cut out to give a working pattern (the method of constructing patterns is given in Chapter 5: Design and Patterns). There is no need to cut a pattern for the belt loop; simply cut a strip 4½ in (113mm) long by ¾in (19mm) wide, then nick off all four corners at 45 degrees. Using a scratch awl, trace the patterns onto the leather. Don't forget to mark the placement of the press stud and the start and end points for the stitching. Carefully cut out the leather.

STEP 2: EDGE SHAVING (BEVELLING)

The general rule for edge shaving is to take off all edges on both grain and flesh sides, except for facing edges that are to be joined. (Working through the remainder of this step should make this statement clearer).

Starting with the back piece, edge shave (bevel) all around the grain side with a No.1 or 2 edge shave. Transfer the start and end points for the stitching to the flesh side. Then shave around the top (the pointed part where the press stud is to be fixed) from one point to the other. The bottom half of the flesh side is not edged as it is to be joined to the front piece. Take the front piece and edge all around the grain side and along the top edge, only on the flesh side.

This now leaves the belt loop. Starting on the grain side, measure 1in (25mm) in from one end and place a mark across the loop. Edge around the long side of the loop starting and finishing at the mark. From the mark, skive the grain side to half its original substance. Turn the loop so the flesh side is uppermost and repeat the process on the opposite end. If done correctly the loop should have one end skived on the grain side and the opposite end skived on the flesh side.

STEP 3: HOLE PUNCHING

Using the correct size of punch to accommodate the stem of the press stud, punch out the holes in the back and front piece (the size of press stud used in this example required a No.4 hole punch). If the project is not going to be dyed, polish all edges using a sealer.

STEP 4: STITCH MARKING

Mark a line $1/3$ in (3mm) in from the edge of the leather on the grain side of all the pieces (back, front and loop strap) using a screw crease or groover. Parts of this line will be used as a guide for the stitch marks while the remainder is for decoration purposes only. If you do not have a screw crease or groover, use a pair of dividers but only mark where the stitching is to go.

PRACTICE PROJECT: Belt Pouch *continued*

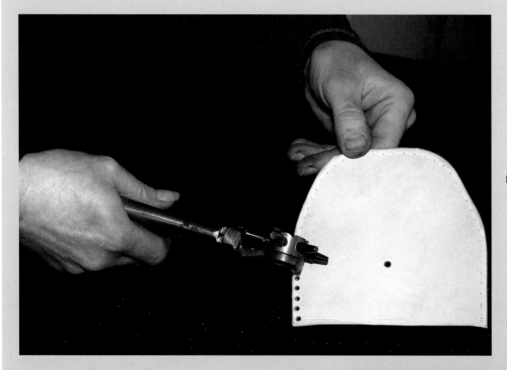

Punching the lace holes using the punch pliers.

Set the dividers to ¼in (6mm). On the back piece, walk the dividers along the line encompassing the bottom part of the piece between the two stitch points. Both sides and the bottom of the front piece are marked in the same manner but not the top. Punch out the marked areas using a No. 1 punch. It is important that the number of punched holes on the front and back pieces are the same, and the spacing between the marks may require adjusting. (If the instructions have been followed correctly there should be 43 holes on both pieces). If the project is to be stitched together rather than laced, stitch mark the front piece only, using a stitch marker.

On the belt loop place two parallel lines of stitch marks 1in (25mm) long on both ends of the loop. The marks should be on the opposite side to the skiving; hence, one pair will be on the grain side and the other on the flesh side. The flesh side will require heavier marking than the grain side as stitch marks on the flesh side can be difficult to see.

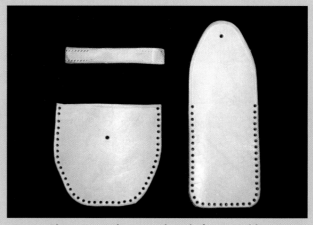

Pieces cut and prepared ready for assembly.

STEP 5: MARKING FOLDS

On the flesh side of the front piece mark two lines to indicate where to fold the leather during moulding. The first line is at a distance of ³⁄₈in (10mm) from the leather's edge and the second at 1³⁄₈in (35mm). Best results are achieved with a groover as the leather naturally wants to follow the groove line when folded.

PRACTICE PROJECT: Belt Pouch *continued*

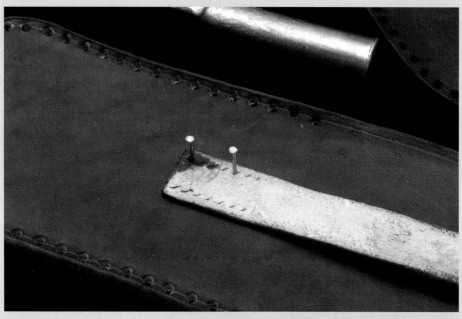

Pinning the top end of the belt loop into place before stitching.

Cleaning and Dyeing

Clean and dye the leather at this stage if required. Do not use leather feeds or antique finish as the wax content will prevent the water from penetrating the leather.

Press Studs

Fit the component parts of the press studs to the front and back pieces.

STEP 6: BELT LOOP STITCHING

The belt loop will be attached to the grain side of the back piece using a saddle stitch (*see* instructions above for saddle stitch and crossing over). Working with the end of the loop that has been stitch marked on the flesh side, position the loop in the centre of the back piece with the first stitch mark on the loop (the stitch mark furthest from the end) roughly in line with the second stitch hole. The long end of the loop should be pointing towards the top of the back piece. Tack panel pins through the stitch marks to hold the loop in place during stitching. Stitch this end of the loop in place, removing the panel pins as necessary; then finish off by hammering the stitching flat.

Fold the loop so that the grain side is visible and the stitch marking is towards the bottom of the back piece. Pin then stitch the loop as previously described.

Pinning the bottom end of the belt loop.

STEP 7: MOULDING

All the moulding is done on the front piece. Make sure that the leather is well dampened. Then working along the first line in from the edge, fold the leather grain to grain (this is to allow the joined edges of the leather to lay flat against each other). Fold the leather along the second line flesh to flesh, to give the shape. Keep the leather well dampened while moulding.

On these types of projects having a pattern to mould around makes life easier. These patterns are known as formers (*see* Chapter 5).

PRACTICE PROJECT: Belt Pouch *continued*

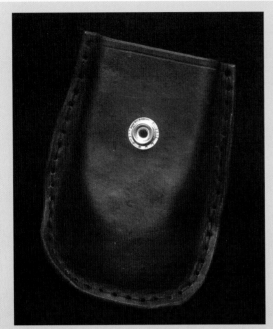

Leather dampened and folded into shape.

Pouch being laced.

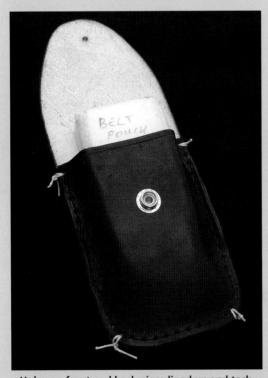

Holes on front and back piece lined up and tack
stitched prior to lacing; the former is left in
place to maintain the shape.

STEP 8: LACING

Lacing is best performed while the leather is still damp.
Line up the stitching holes and lace the two pieces together using either the double or triple loop stitch (the
example has used the triple loop stitch). Approximately
8ft (2.5m) of lacing will be required to complete the stitch
run in one continuous length.

To stitch, use a saddle stitch; the first and last stitches
should go over the end of the front piece.

This piece should not be placed in the clams unless a
former has been made and placed between the front and
back pieces; otherwise the tension of the clam jaws would
crush the leather, resulting in possible creases.

PRACTICE PROJECT: Belt Pouch *continued*

STEP 9: FINISHING MOULDING

Often in the process of working the leather some of the desired shape will be lost. Dampen the leather and mould it into shape using your fingers, pack the inside with newspaper or use the former if available; this will maintain the shape of the pouch while drying. Allow to dry naturally away from any direct heat source. When nearly dry remove the former or any newspaper to allow air to circulate around the inside of the pouch. When dry, use a good quality leather feed to polish and feed the leather.

TACK STITCHES

Tack stitches are individual stitches placed at strategic points around the work to temporarily hold two pieces together while a more permanent fixing is made. Beginners may find it easier to place three or four tack stitches around the work to hold it together while being laced. As the corners are rounded there is no need to go through the three corner holes twice, as in the above description of the double and triple loop stitches. If the pieces are to be stitched together, tack stitches are essential to ensure the two pieces line up.

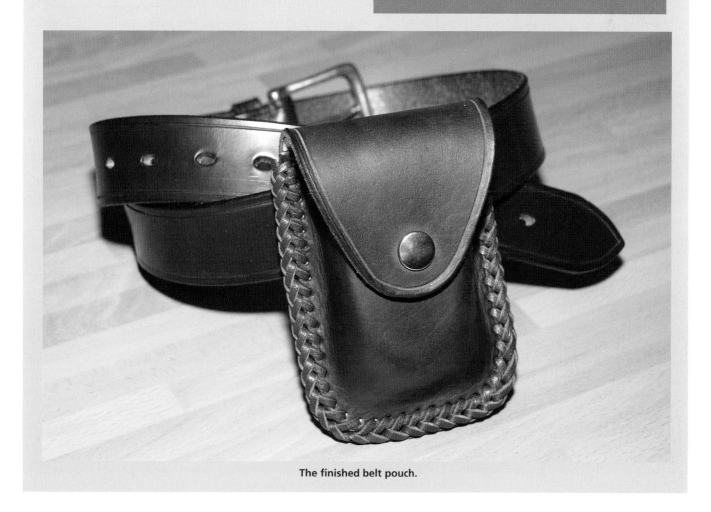

The finished belt pouch.

An array of different types of straps.

CHAPTER 4

STRAP MAKING

Making straps is a very important part of leatherwork. It incorporates techniques for attaching buckles and making fixed and running keepers. Many leather items will have some form of strap incorporated within their construction, and it is unlikely that you could go through your leatherworking career without making straps. The core business of many leather workshops is based on strap making, such as belts, dog collars and leads.

There are two sizes that you need to be familiar with, the made-up and cut sizes. The made-up size is the required size when the strap is fastened. The cut size is the actual length that the leather is cut to, i.e. the made-up size plus all allowances.

The part where the leather folds over the furnishing, e.g. ring, buckle, hook, is called the return. When making a strap always make up the return on the best end of the strap (*see* Chapter 2); this ensures that the buckle is on the strongest part of the leather. Do not edge shave the portion of the return where the two flesh sides meet when the leather is folded – this allows the edges of the join to lie flush; if they were edged there would be a groove where the two pieces of leather joined. When stitching rings into returns, it is better to use a ring with a diameter size ¼in (6mm) wider, or larger, than the width of the return. If the same size was used the edges of the ring would cut into the edges of the leather.

Straps should have an uneven number of holes, and a correctly fitting strap should fasten on the centre hole with an even number of holes either side. Hence the made-up size is measured from the centre of the crew hole (where the leather folds if the strap is made up) to the middle hole. This is not a safety issue; it is so that the strap looks balanced when fastened.

The following conventions are meant as a guide, and discretion is required especially when working with very wide or narrow straps. Try to keep a picture of the end product in mind and adjust the distances accordingly.

Strap Length and Position of Holes

The position of the first hole from the end of the strap should be three times the width of the strap. The distance between the holes should be the same as the width of the strap. These extra measurements need to be added to the made-up size to obtain the cut size.

CALCULATING STRAP LENGTH AND HOLE POSITION

EXAMPLE:
A person with a waist measurement of 32in (81.25cm) has commissioned a 1in (25mm) wide belt. We have decided to use a buckle return length of 2in (50mm) and to have five holes.

The made-up size will be 32in (81.25cm) = *The actual waist size*
The cut size is calculated like this:
- 32in (82cm) *made-up size*
- + 2in (50mm) *for the buckle return*
- + 3in (80mm) *the distance from front of belt to first hole (3 times belt width)* The correct fastening position is on the centre hole; therefore two holes will be in front of the fastening position. The width of the belt is 1in (25mm) which equals the spacing between the holes.
- + 2in (50mm)

Therefore the cut size: will be 39in (100cm).

Returns

The return is the distance from the end of the leather to where the leather is to be folded to accommodate furnishings. When buckles are to be attached this is also known as the *buckle return* and refers to the distance from the end of the leather to the centre of the crew hole.

The length of a return will depend on the type of leather being used, the weight (thickness) and number of furnishings to be attached (for example, dog collars require keepers and a D-ring to attach the lead to), and the amount of strain that will be placed upon the strap. A 2in (50mm) return would suffice for a belt; however the return on the breeching on a horse harness would be 4–5in (101–127mm). When calculating the length of a return, add an extra ½in (12mm) to allow for the fold of the leather around the furnishing.

After skiving the returns on a strap, always nick off a small amount of the corners at 45 degrees. The reason for this is that sharp corners tend to catch and fold away from the join; this not only leaves an uneven surface but over time the leather or stitching could be torn.

The two main methods used to secure returns are riveting or stitching. Occasionally on buckle returns press studs are used, which allows the buckle to be easily swapped. The procedure for securing a return around a furnishing such as a trigger hook is the same as that for attaching a buckle, the only difference being that the crew hole is not punched. We will concentrate on the attachment of buckles here, as the procedure is slightly more involved.

Always nick off the corners of returns.

Initial Preparation

Regardless of how the buckle is to be attached, preparation of the strap to receive the buckle is unchanged.

Mark the position of the return in the centre of the strap on the grain side. Position the centre of the crew punch over the mark and in the middle of the strap with the 'slot' running parallel to the edges. Crew holes that are off line look dreadful; to avoid this initially tap the punch lightly and then remove it. An impression of the punch will be made on the leather which will give an indication as to how accurate you have been. Replace the crew punch adjusting the position if necessary and punch the hole.

In practice the skiving is performed as one action, but for ease of description it has been broken down into two parts. The first part is to skive from the front of the crew hole towards the end of the leather on the flesh side. It should be tapered gradually leaving approximately a quarter of the original substance at the end. When complete, turn the leather so that the grain is upmost; tidy it as necessary and nick off the corners at 45 degrees.

The second part of the process is to skive down the crew hole itself. Removing a thin shaving will aid in the folding of the leather around the buckle. However, there will be occasions when you need to remove more of the substance. This will depend on the type of buckle being used, the width and functionality of the strap and the substance of the leather. As a rule the smaller the buckle the less room there is to accommodate the leather. A little judgement is required. The crew hole needs to be skived down enough to be aesthetically pleasing but not so thin as to break when the item is used.

Edge shave around the inside of the crew hole with a No. 4 edge shave. (Use the largest available if you do not possess a No. 4.) This enables the tongue of the buckle to sit right into the crew hole. Position the buckle in the crew hole and fold the leather around the buckle bar (the strip of metal to which the tongue is attached) flesh to flesh.

POSITIONING CREW PUNCH

Push the punch into the leather to make an impression.

Check the position and adjust as necessary (the impression has been exaggerated for clarity).

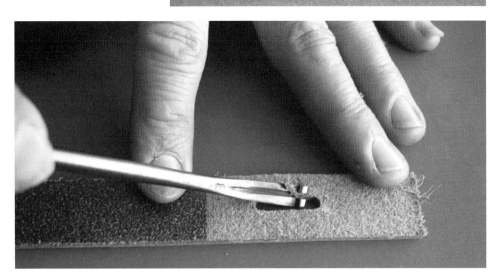

Edge shaving around the inside of crew holes allows the buckle tongue to sit snugly into the return.

FOLDING HEAVY LEATHERS

LEFT:
Dampen the end of the fold.

BELOW (MIDDLE):
Fold the leather grain to grain
to stretch the grain surface.

BELOW (BOTTOM):
Complete the fold; stretching the
grain surface helps to prevent it
from cracking when folded.

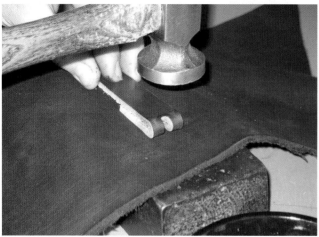

Folding the Leather

A little care needs to be exercised when folding the leather as there is a danger of cracking the grain; this is especially true on heavier and dyed leathers. To avoid this, before the buckle is placed into position, fold the leather back on itself, grain to grain; dampen the fold and tap it with a hammer; this stretches the grain. Fold it back the correct way, flesh to flesh, and again tap with a hammer. (Note: Just a light tap will do. Avoid being heavy handed.)

Securing the Return

RIVETED RETURN

To prevent excessive movement of the buckle and the end of the return folding away from the join, the rivets need to be as close to the buckle and the end of the return as possible. Consequently the returns for riveted buckles are somewhat shorter than their stitched counterparts. The number of rivets used will depend on the project. On narrower straps one rivet may be sufficient, while wider straps would require two or possibly three. When using several rivets, ensure that they are in line.

With the buckle in position, mark the position of the rivets on the grain surface, then punch out the holes using an appropriately sized punch. Punching out both layers of the fold together will ensure that the holes are in line, but take care that the leather does not move. Rivet the piece together as described in Chapter 3.

STITCHED RETURN

This task is a bit more involved and takes a little practice, but to my mind neatly stitched returns look more professional than riveted returns (in the equestrian trade returns are never riveted). Bear in mind that the narrower the strap the more difficult it is to stitch in the buckle, especially when keepers are involved.

The stitching needs to start as close to the buckle as possible. With the buckle in place, with your thumbnail mark both edges of the strap just behind the buckle bar, then repeat the process to mark the end of the return; the stitch marking will go between these two marks on either side of the strap.

Remove the buckle and lay the strap on the bench. Stitch mark between the marks on either side of the strap. The stitch marks need to be close to the edge of the leather but not so close that the awl breaks through the edge when stitching. Approximately $1/16$in (1.5mm) on straps $3/4$in (19mm) and narrower and $1/8$in (3mm) on wider straps. Replace the buckle and stitch into place.

It is easier to pull the leather directly behind a buckle bar together using an overstitch than the securing stitch. However, on certain projects this may not be appropriate so a double stitch would be required. Whichever is used will be down to aesthetics and judgement.

Keepers (Loops)

A keeper is a loop through which the leather is passed to hold it in place. A range of metal keepers can be purchased with either plain or fancy finishes or made from leather. A *fixed keeper* sits directly behind the buckle, while a *running keeper* is free to slide along the strap.

Leather Keepers

It is best to make these up in a continuous strip (known as looping) and cut them to length as required. Look through

Riveted buckle returns.

STITCH MARKING RETURNS

Position the buckle and use the thumbnail to mark behind the buckle bar and the end of the return.

Stitch mark between the marked areas on both sides.

Marking the length of a running keeper.

Running keeper prepared for stitching; pliers placed in the stitching clams are used to hold the keeper together prior to stitching.

the scrap box for suitable pieces, and keep any unused lengths for later projects. The width of the keeper will depend on the width of the strap, and on what you think will look good. On a ½in (12mm) strap, a keeper ³/₈in (10mm) wide would be in keeping, but on a 1½in (37mm) wide belt the same width would be lost.

Trying to fold leather ¹/₈in (3mm) in substance around a ¾in (19mm) buckle would be very difficult, and the keeper would look cumbersome on the strap; therefore, the sub-

stance requires reducing, either on the splitting machine (if you are lucky enough to have one) or with the skiver. It needs to be thin enough to fold around the strap but not so thin that it will break after a few uses. Remove a little at a time, periodically testing it on the strap, until the required substance is obtained.

A keeper should snugly grip the leather being passed through it, and getting the size correct can take a little practice.

RUNNING KEEPERS

To measure the length of the running keeper, place one edge of the looping against one side of the strap, then wrap it tightly around the strap, overlapping the looping. On wide straps a maximum of 1in (25mm) of overlap will be sufficient. Riveted keepers will only require enough overlap to accommodate the diameter of the rivet to be used. As the leather will make a loop, you will need to wrap the keeper around a solid object such as a metal loop stick while you are riveting it.

Slacken the looping by an amount slightly less than the thickness of the leather to be passed through it; mark the position using your thumbnail and cut it to size. Skive the grain side on one end of the keeper and the flesh side on the other. The idea is to have a continuous thickness when the two ends are joined. If a number of keepers are required for the same width of strap, use this as a pattern to cut the desired quantity. Always use the original as the pattern, otherwise any cutting errors will be accumulated. It would be prudent for beginners to only cut one extra keeper, make it up and check the fit before cutting the remainder. It is heart breaking to find that you have ten keepers all cut too short.

Now either stitch or rivet the keeper together. Riveting is a simple case of overlapping the ends to the desired amount and securing with the rivet.

If stitching the keeper together, place a line of stitch marking on both sides corresponding to the amount of overlap; on narrow straps this will only be two or three marks. Place the keeper into the loop clams and stitch together using a back stitch. An alternative to using loop clams is to grip the keeper with a pair of pliers and place these into the clams.

As there is very little wear on a keeper and the thread will be out of sight, when crossing over make the last stitch over the end of the join, then pass the needle between the loop of the keeper to the other side. Similarly only the last stitch requires strengthening when finishing.

FIXED KEEPERS

As with running keepers wrap the looping tightly around the strap, only this time the required length will be where the looping meets the end. Adjust for the thickness, mark and cut. If you are unsure it is better to leave the keeper too long, as it can be adjusted while being fixed.

The keeper needs to be as close to the buckle as possible. Stitch mark the strap as described, and do the first stitch. Prick out the number of stitch marks corresponding to the width of the keeper (normally three or four). Remove the strap from

Position the keeper and stitch the first side as normal.

Place the first stitch as normal.

Stitch marks inaccessible from the front can be stitched from the back following previously pre-pricked holes; moving the keeper to one side allows access.

Blocking up fixed and running keepers.

Different strap ends: (left) bridle point; (right) egg point.

the clams and position the keeper between the two layers of leather, against the first stitch with the end slightly above the centre of the strap and the flesh side facing the direction in which it is to be turned. Push the awl through the pricked-out stitch hole ensuring that it catches the keeper (this holds the keeper in place) and return the work to the clams.

Ensuring that the keeper is at 90 degrees to the strap, stitch in the normal manner, crossing over and stopping before the keeper. Prick out the stitch marks and push the keeper between the two layers of leather as far as it will go. If the keeper is too big cut a small amount off the end and try it again.

By manipulating the keeper it is possible to follow the awl through with the needles in the normal manner. If you find that a stitch mark cannot be reached from the front of the work, locate the corresponding mark on the back of the work with the awl (it should have been pricked out) and push it through, being careful not to pierce the keeper. Move the keeper to one side (it may be necessary to push the awl further through once this has been done) and withdraw the awl, following it through with the needle to complete the stitch. This is one of the few times we stitch from the front first.

It is easier to position the keeper and keep it in place if the stitch immediately before the keeper is initially not tightened. When the first stitch through the keeper is pulled tight it should also tighten the prior stitch.

Metal keepers are fixed in the same manner. Obviously they cannot be stitched through; instead make a long stitch over the metal.

Strictly speaking only fixed keepers are stitched in place, but riveted returns may also require 'fixed' keepers. To achieve this, make a running keeper or use a metal keeper. Rivet the return as close to the buckle as possible. Slip the keeper between the two pieces of leather, pushing it up to the rivets. Then rivet the return again directly behind the keeper.

BLOCKING UP

This is a technique employed to give the keepers a box shape, and although not essential it gives the project a more professional finish. Select the loop stick corresponding to the width of the strap and push it through the keeper. Shape the keeper by tapping around the flat surfaces with the harness hammer or equivalent. Do not tap the cornered edges, as the cornered edges of the loop stick could cut through the keeper if struck and there is also the possibility of damaging the stick itself. With fixed keepers leave the loop stick in place and tap the stitching on the back flat. Running a hot crease around the keeper looks neater and helps to maintain its shape.

Strap Ends

The end of the strap could be left square, but a nicely made strap end will only add to the appearance of the finished product. The most commonly used strap ends are the egg point, rounded point and bridle point.

Egg Points and Rounded Points

The simplest method of cutting these is to use a strap end chisel; however it is possible to cut both of these by hand. The egg point is relatively easy to cut given a little practice, but to cut a neat round point is very difficult and it would be better to use the chisel or consider using an egg point.

CUTTING AN EGG POINT

On the grain side mark the end of the strap in the centre. Holding the strap, place the strap end on the end of the bench with the grain side upmost – there should be approximately the width of the strap plus $^1/_8$ in (3mm) on the bench. Place the round knife against the edge of the leather close to the bench. Pull the leather into the knife and at the same time roll the knife forward. Aim to finish on the centre mark. Turn the

leather over (flesh side uppermost) and repeat the process starting the cut directly opposite the first cut. The trick is to keep your eye on the centre mark. Finish by tidying the edges with sandpaper.

A word of warning: This does tend to take gouges out of the bench, so place the leather on a scrap piece of wood making sure that it is secured. Do not attempt this on the dining room table or the kitchen work surfaces!

BRIDLE POINTS

There are no hard and fast rules on cutting these points. Yet again it comes down to judgement and aesthetics. Here are a few guidelines, however, that will give you a good starting point.

Referring to the bridle point illustration, the distance between A and B is the width of the strap. The distance between C and D will vary depending on the strap width. For widths $^3/_4$ in (19mm) and under, use $^1/_{16}$ in (1.5mm). For $^3/_4$–1$^1/_4$ in (19–31mm) use $^1/_8$ in (3mm). For any width above this use $^1/_4$ in (6mm).

To construct the point, measure and mark distances A to B then distances C to D; draw a line connecting points A to D. Carefully cut along the lines, then nick off the corners at 45 degrees. Use sandpaper to round off point A.

CUTTING AN EGG POINT

Place the strap on the edge of the bench with the round knife at the start of the cut.

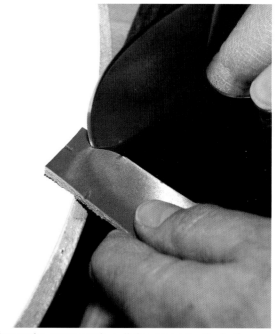

Aiming at the centre mark, pull the strap into the knife, simultaneously rolling the knife forward.

CUTTING AN EGG POINT

Turn the strap over and repeat the process.

Completed egg point.

How to cut a bridal point.

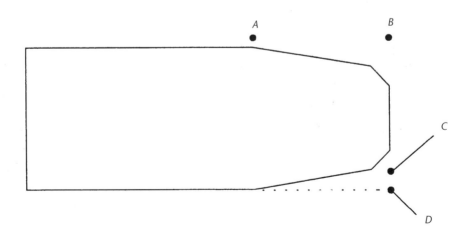

PRACTICE PROJECT

Plain Belt

The best way to practise strap making is to make a plain belt. The techniques used are employed on any kind of strap, and as belts are normally relatively wide, beginners will find the stitching of buckles and keepers easier. Almost any kind of leather can be used to make a belt, but the better the quality of leather the better the finished product will be. If you wish to decorate the belt by tooling or colouring then you will have to use natural vegetable tanned leather.

In this project we have assumed the use of a $^1/_8$– $^3/_{16}$in (3.5–4mm) vegetable tanned leather. The actual dimensions have not been supplied as it is envisaged that you will probably wish to make this belt to fit yourself or family member. Likewise, the techniques may need adjusting to suit your choice of materials (e.g. sealing the edges rather than edge dying if natural vegetable tanned leather is used). All the information required to make this belt has been discussed in this and previous chapters.

The processes involved in making this belt are relevant to any type of strap and hopefully will demonstrate that the major part of the time expended on a project is spent in the preparation. Do not cut corners. The end result will only be as good as the preparation.

NOT SURE WHAT LENGTH?

If you are unsure of the cut length, prepare the buckle return as described leaving the strip uncut. Measure the distance of the made-up size from the centre of the crew hole and place a mark on the centre of the strip; this will be the position of the middle buckle hole. Set the dividers to the required distance and mark the required number of holes on either side of the mark. Add the allowance from the last hole to the end of the leather and cut the strip. This method also ensures that the middle hole is in the correct position.

STEP 1: CUT TO LENGTH

Before starting make sure that the leather has a straight edge to work from. Cut a strip of leather to the desired width and square off the best end. Working from this end, measure and cut the required length. Cut a length of looping to an appropriate width and split it down to a workable substance. (Looping of ½in (12mm) works well on straps 1in (25mm) and above in width.) You will need enough looping to make a fixed and running keeper.

STEP 2: BUCKLE RETURN

On the best end of the strap, mark the position of the crew hole and punch it out. 2in (50mm) returns are fairly standard for stitched returns on belts 1in (25mm) wide and above. Skive the return, nick off the corners and edge shave the inside of the crew hole.

STEP 3: STRAP END

On the opposite end of the strap, cut a point of your choosing. Mark the position of the first buckle hole in the centre of the strap, set the dividers to the required spacing and by walking them up the centre of the strap, mark the remaining holes. Five holes is the norm on belts, but if you wish to place more, remember to have an uneven number and to include the extra allowance when calculating the cut size. Punch out the holes using the appropriate size punch.

STEP 4: EDGE SHAVING

Edge shaving is best performed with a No. 2 edge shave. On the grain side, edge shave around the whole piece. On the flesh side do not edge where the return is joined. Fold the return to its desired position, then using your thumbnail, mark a line across the strap at the end of the return. Edge shave the flesh side leaving the area above the line (the return) untouched. Edge shave the grain and flesh sides of the looping.

STEP 5: GROOVING

On our belt we have used a groover to make a decorative line around the belt as it gives a more permanent impression. It will also serve as a guide for the stitch marks. If you wish to use a crease, do this after the strap has been edge dyed (Step 6). Set the groover to an appropriate width and groove all around the grain side.

PRACTICE PROJECT: Plain Belt *continued*

GROOVING AFTER EDGE SHAVING

You may wonder why the grooving or creasing is done after the edge shaving, since before edge shaving we have a nice square edge to work from. If it was done first, there is a danger of cutting into the line with the edge shave. Done after, the groover or crease can be set to avoid the shaved edge.

If you are unsure of what width to set the groover or crease, test it on the area between the crew hole and the end of the leather. This section will be folded underneath and out of sight when the project is complete.

STEP 6: EDGE DYING

Dye and polish all the edges and the skived end of the return. Use a pipe cleaner to dye the crew hole and groove line (if used). Polish the crew hole and groove line using a pointed bone or any other appropriate implement (the end of a fine paint brush works well). Do not forget to dye the edges and skived areas of the looping.

Apply any crease lines after all edge dying has been performed. The crease line could be rubbed out during the polishing process if applied before edge dying. If the keepers are to be blocked up, do not crease the looping.

Cut a fixed and a running keeper to length. Skive the relevant areas of the running keeper and dye these areas.

STEP 7: STITCHING MARKING

Stitch mark the buckle return at 7 or 8 stitches per inch (25mm). If a groove line was used, mark directly into the line. With crease lines, position the stitch marks so that the top of the stitch marks just touch the bottom of the crease line. Stitch mark the running keeper.

STEP 8: CONSTRUCTION

Use an 18/4 or 18/5 thread. Stitch the running keeper using a single hand stitch. Position the buckle and stitch the return using a saddle stitch; not forgetting to place the fixed keeper. Beginners may find it easier to pull the leather behind the buckle together if an over stitch is used to secure the first stitch.

QUICK EDGE DYEING

Edge dyeing long lengths of looping can be made easier by rolling it tightly together.

Edge dyeing long lengths of looping can be an arduous task. Roll the looping into a tight circle with the flesh side out. Apply the dye to one side, turn it over and dye the other side. Unroll the looping, polish the edges then dye the flesh side.

STEP 9: FINISHING

Block up and crease the keepers. Re-dye and polish the areas where the leather has been joined so that it looks like one piece. If a crease line has been used, re-crease over the stitching. Finally, feed and polish with a good quality leather feed.

Re-dyeing and polishing a finished join.

Raised Straps

The appearance of any strap can be enhanced if it is raised to give it a slightly rounded appearance. The technique can only be done on lined straps, and is achieved by skiving down the edges of the strap and lining. (Lined straps are made up of two strips of leather; the strip on the bottom is known as the lining.) A more pronounced raise can be achieved by placing a fillet (a thin piece of leather) between the two pieces of leather. If this technique is used, the fillet should not extend into the buckle return or the area where the buckle holes are to be punched.

Obviously this will make the strap much thicker, and beginners are advised to use it only on straps that are 1in (50mm) in width or wider. On narrower straps this technique takes a lot of practice, and the correct choice of buckle is es-sential as many will not have sufficient clearance to accom-modate the extra thickness.

When calculating the cut sizes for these types of straps it is advisable to add an extra ½in (12mm) to accommodate the extra thickness when in use.

Raised Dog Collar

Use a good quality shoulder with a minimum of 3mm (1/8in) substance or better. You will also require a D-ring and buckle. As there is stitching across the grain, use a large stitch length, 6 per inch (25mm), and 18/5 or 18/6 thread. Actual dimen-sions have not been given as each individual will have differ-ing requirements.

Raised dog collar dimensions.

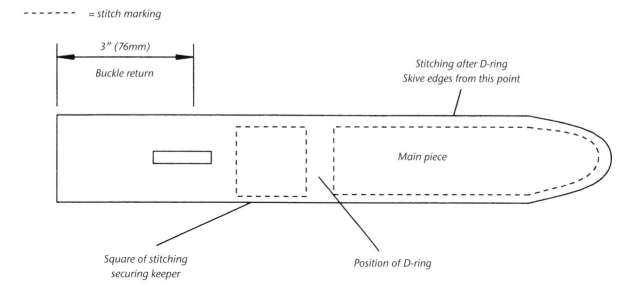

- - - - - - = stitch marking

3" (76mm)

Buckle return

Stitching after D-ring
Skive edges from this point

Main piece

Square of stitching
securing keeper

Position of D-ring

Cut the lining approx. 2" (50mm) longer than the main piece

End view of straps
Taper ½" (12mm)
towards centre

STRAP PREPARATION

Cut and prepare the pieces in the normal manner, initially putting the lining to one side. Observe the following:

■ Skive the end of the return down to virtually nothing.
■ Do not punch out the buckle holes.
■ Do not edge shave the flesh side or from ½in (12mm) behind the crew hole to the end of the return. The lining will overlap this area.
■ Only the length of the return will require edge dyeing. The remaining edges will be dyed once the strap is put together. If very heavy leathers are used the substance may require reducing. In this instance do not dye the flesh side.
■ Stitch mark in accordance with the illustration.

A groove line is best employed; making it slightly deeper will allow the stitches to sit below the leather surface, thus reducing wear.

Fold and mark the end of the return. Starting and ending at this point, use a skiver or skirt shave to reduce the two sides and strap point of the strap (on the flesh side) to approximately one third of its original thickness. The taper should extend about ½in (12mm) towards the centre. (This distance is reduced or increased depending on the width of the strap.)

LINING PREPARATION

Depending on the type of leather being used, reduce the substance of the lining, on the flesh side, by approximately half. Skive one end down to approximately a quarter of its original substance and nick off the corners; make sure that the edge shave is run across this end.

With the groover set to the same distance used on the strap, place a groove line on either side of the lining; edge dye in the normal manner but do not dye the flesh side. Use the skirt shave or skiver to reduce the two sides of the flesh side to approximately half of their remaining thickness.

CONSTRUCTION

Provisionally the strap and the lining need to be fastened together prior to stitching. This is best done by gluing and pinning.

1. Position the buckle and glue the return.
2. Position the keeper and pin it into place.

3. Position the D-ring and glue the lining to the strap ensuring that the edges are in line (glue flesh side to flesh side). The skived end of the lining should be positioned so that there will be one stitch over its end. The lining will extend past the strap point; this is to allow for the accurate positioning of the point and will be cut off once the pieces are stitched.
4. Looking at the strap lengthwise with the buckle furthest away from you, place pins at intervals along the left side of the strap. Pin into the stitch marks and try to get the pins straight and coming out in the groove line on the lining. This way the holes will be covered by the stitching. Pushing an awl through prior to placing the pin makes this easier.
5. Using a saddle stitch, first stitch in the keeper, then stitch the remaining length. Angle the awl so that the stitches are in the groove line on the lining.

When the lining and the strap are glued together, there should be a gap between them along both sides. As the two are stitched and pulled together the gap is closed and the raise is formed.

FINISHING

Cut the excess lining to match the strap point. Then punch out the holes using a No.23 oval or No.6 round punch. Given the weight of these straps it helps if the holes are punched twice; once from the front, then also from the back.

Use the skiver to tidy any uneven areas. Ensure that the skiver is held at 90 degrees to the edge, and take care not to cut the stitching. When the edges are flush, go back round them with the edge shave, then dye and polish the edges.

Block up the keeper, then place the strap face down in the appropriate groove on the rolling block. Tapping the strap with the harness hammer pushes it into the groove, which helps to shape it and flatten the stitching. Finally feed and polish.

PROTECT YOUR WORK

Over time, lead blocks and other punching surfaces can become quite rough. Protect the surface of your work piece by placing a piece of scrap leather between it and the punching surface.

A raised strap being shaped in the rolling block.

Raised Belt (Using Fillet)

Cut and prepare a belt and lining to your own specifications using the techniques described. However, reduce the strap by two thirds of its original substance and do not skive down the sides of the strap and lining. Cut a fillet ½in (12mm) narrower than the belt width and cut to length. It should start behind the end of the return and finish 2in (50mm) in front of the last buckle hole (the last hole from the strap end). Reduce the substance by half (adjust reduction to suit) and skive around all four sides of the grain surface to virtually nothing.

Position the buckle and keeper and glue the return. Place the strap on the bench with the flesh side uppermost; then place the lining below it, positioning it as it would be when stitched. Mark the position of the fillet onto the lining (drawing a line down the centre will aid positioning) and glue the fillet into place.

Glue and pin the two pieces together and stitch. Due to the depth of the fillet, the lining may slightly overlap when stitched together; trim the excess and finish as normal.

Plaiting

Plaiting can be used to great effect on handles for bags, dog collars and leads, wrist bands – in fact, any type of single strap can be plaited. Plaiting patterns range from simple to very complex, which are beyond the scope of this book; here we will be concentrating on the simpler types of plait.

Plaiting can be either open or closed ended. An open end plait is where one end of an item is made up (such as the strap end of a dog collar), then the remaining leather is split into strands and plaited; a piece of leather is then stitched over the loose end of plait (normally a buckle return). A closed end plait is where the two ends of the leather are left intact and the strands are made by splitting the leather between them.

Closed Ended Plaits

These types of plait will amaze your friends; you can guarantee that someone will take it apart and not be able to put it back together again. The secret is in the way the leather is crossed and twisted to make up one unit of plait. This sequence is then repeated to plait the remaining length of the strap, and on long plaits it is easy to become confused. It helps to mentally number each strand and say the sequence to yourself as you work.

As the plait progresses, the overall length will be reduced. The actual amount will depend on the leather substance, the width of the strands and how tight the plait is made. As a rough guide, on $\frac{1}{8}$in (3mm) natural tanned leather, one unit of plaiting with $\frac{1}{4}$in (6mm) strands would require a strand length of 5$\frac{1}{2}$in (139mm); $\frac{1}{2}$in (12mm) would be lost from the overall length.

Using these figures, if a belt had a plaited length of 16$\frac{1}{2}$in (42cm), there would be three complete units of plaiting; therefore, length would be reduced by 1$\frac{1}{2}$in (37mm), leaving an overall length of 15in (38cm). Reference to the overall length in this example is to the plaited area only. Obviously if a plaited belt was being made, the buckle return and strap end would also have to be taken into consideration. The best advice when making long items is to cut the strands short, make the plait, re-measure and adjust accordingly. The strands can always be lengthened but not shortened.

Preparing the straps for plaiting involves cutting and edge shaving relatively thin strands, which can prove awkward. Exercise extreme care. Placing the strap against the edge of a ruler will help to steady it while being worked. All dyeing and finishing of the plaited area must be done before the plait is constructed.

For 3- and 5-strand plaits, reference the plaiting sequence photographs; for ease of explanation and clarity on the photographs, each strand has been coloured. Obviously it is not possible to colour the strands of a project, so mentally substitute each colour for a number. Start by holding the strap vertically with the Blue strand on your left, as you look at it. Hence, Blue would be No.1, Green 2 and Red 3 and so on; the numbered sequence will be given in brackets at the end of each instruction. Always work from the front; the plaiting is done at the top and the twisting at the bottom. At the end of the plait it can be quite difficult to perform the final twist; make the plaits tight to allow more room at the end, the spacing can be adjusted once the plait is complete.

3- and 5-strand plait dimensions.

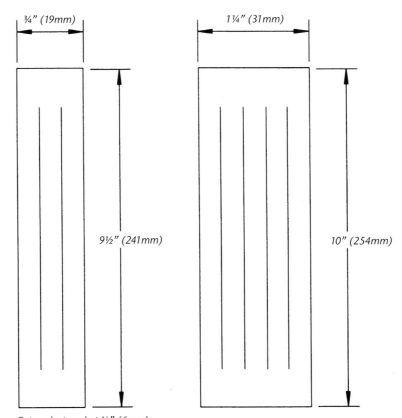

¾" (19mm)   1¼" (31mm)

9½" (241mm)   10" (254mm)

Cut each strand at ¼" (6mm)
Allow ¾" (19mm) on each end for press stud

3-STRANDED PLAIT

The dimensions given are based on ⅛in (3mm) thick natural vegetable leather and will accommodate 1½ units of plaiting. The finished length will be 8½in (215mm), and by placing a press stud on either end it can be used as a wrist band.

Cut the leather to the dimensions given and nick off the corners. Set the dividers to ¼in (6mm) and mark a line on either side of the strap; if the strip was cut accurately the centre strand should also be ¼in (6mm). Carefully cut the strands. Edge shave all edges on both flesh and grain sides, including the strands, and perform any dyeing, feeding and polishing at this point (feeding and polishing is difficult once the plait has been assembled).

1. Cross Blue over Green, then Red over Blue. Twist between Blue and Red above the point where they cross. (Number sequence: 1 over 2, 3 over 1, and twist between 1 and 3 over cross.)
2. Cross Green over Red, Blue over Green, then Red over Blue. Twist between Blue and Green. (Number sequence: 2 over 3, 1 over 2, 3 over 1, and twist between 1 and 2.)
3. Cross Blue over Green, then Red over Blue. Twist between Blue and Green above the point where they cross. (Number sequence: 1 over 2, 3 over 1, then twist between 1 and 2 over cross.)
4. Cross Green over Red, Blue over Green, then Red over Blue. Twist between Green and Blue. (Number sequence: 2 over 3, 1 over 2, 3 over 1, and twist between 1 and 2.)

This is now one complete unit of plaiting. To complete the wrist band, repeat points 1 and 2.

3-STRAND PLAIT SEQUENCE

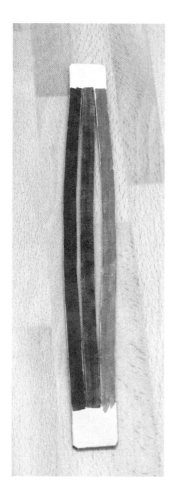

3-STRAND PLAIT SEQUENCE *continued*

5-STRAND PLAIT SEQUENCE

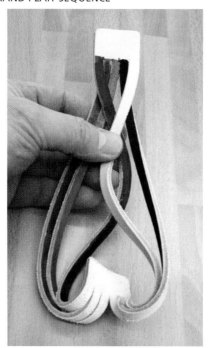

5-STRANDED PLAIT

Although this looks more complicated than the 3-stranded plait, there are actually only two sequences to remember. The dimensions are based on ⅛in (3mm) thick natural vegetable leather and will accommodate two units of plaiting. The finished length will be 9in (229mm) and again, it can be used as a wrist band.

Cut the leather to the given dimensions and nick off the corners. Set the dividers to ¼in (6mm) and mark a line down both sides of the strap. Reset the dividers to ½in (12mm) and repeat the process. This should leave five equal strands. Carefully cut the strands; edge shave, dye and polish as with the 3-stranded plait.

1. Cross Blue over Green and Red, then Natural over Black and Blue. Twist between Red and Black below the point where Natural and Blue cross. (Number sequence: 1 over 2 and 3, 5 over 4 and 1, then twist between 3 and 4.)
2. Cross Green over Red and Natural, Black over Blue and Green, then Red over Natural and Black. Natural and Black should be on the left and Red, Green and Blue on the right. Twist between the resulting gap, above the point where they cross. (Number sequence: 2 over 3 and 5, 4 over 1 and 2, 3 over 5 and 4, then twist into resulting gap.)

This is one complete unit, repeat Points 1 and 2 to complete the wrist band.

PRACTICE PROJECT

Plaited Belt (5-Strand)

Plaited belt dimensions.

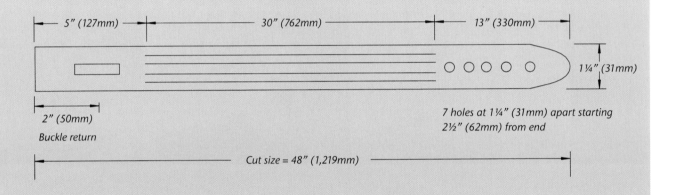

In this project we have used a $^1/_8$–$^3/_{16}$in (3.5–4mm) bridle butt, which can be substituted with a good quality 3mm thick vegetable tanned leather. The dimensions given will fit a 36in (91.5cm) waist to the centre hole. (If you wish to substitute your own dimensions, the length of the plait will require increasing or decreasing.) For reasons that will be discussed at the appropriate juncture, the buckle will need to be ¼in (6mm) narrower than the cut width of the strap.

Because the leather has been cut into individual strands, plaited items tend to stretch more than their plain counterparts. Therefore, it is a good idea to leave enough space between the last buckle hole and the plaiting so that an extra hole can be punched if required.

Cut the leather to the dimensions given plus ½in (12mm) length of looping. Initially, only the area to be plaited and the looping are prepared. Edge shave and dye all edges of the cut strands and the looping. Starting from the strap end, plait the belt in accordance with the instructions already discussed. With the given dimensions there should be seven complete units of plaiting.

It will be noticed that the plait looks narrower than the ends of the leather. To keep the proportions, the two ends will need to be reduced by ¼in (6mm). An equal amount needs to be removed from either side of the strap. Therefore, set the dividers to $^1/_8$in (3mm) and mark a line on both sides of the buckle return and the strap end; go slightly over the outer strands so that when cut the belt looks like a continuous width.

Prepare the remainder of the belt (i.e. edge shave, edge dye, crease or groove and stitch mark). Position the buckle and keeper, then stitch into place. Finish in the normal manner.

Rolled Straps

Done correctly, rolled straps can be more elegant than plain straps, and if used as bag handles they are more comfortable in the hand. There are various methods employed in making rolled straps. The most common is to use a thin leather, wrap it around a filler such as a piece of cord, and stitch along the top. The problem with this method is that the ends require re-enforcing to take the stresses and strains of usage. A stronger method is to use heavier leather and roll the full substance. Other processes involve wrapping strips of leather around a fillet.

When rolling leather, there are a few basic guidelines to follow. When finished, the stitching should appear as a continuous length with the ends of the returns tucked into the rolled part. In general, the rolled part will be wider than the ends; therefore, the ends will require shaping. Any furnishings will need to be stitched into place first.

Rolled Bag Handle

The given dimensions can be altered to suit your needs, but bear in mind that the thinner the strap, the more difficult it is to roll. As a lot of strain will be placed on the thread when pulling the rolled area together, use a 18/5 or 18/6 thread. Cut a strip of leather 1½in (37mm) wide, then shape the leather to the dimensions given. Edge shave the grain side only. Then set the groover to ⅛in (3mm) and place a groove line around the grain side (a deep groove line is better than a crease line as it allows the stitching to sit below the leather surface). Skive, edge dye (only the returns and groove lines require edge dyeing) and stitch mark in accordance with the illustration.

To aid in the rolling of the leather, remove a thin layer of leather from the flesh side and place three groove lines along the length of the rolled area: one in the centre, then one either side, central to the leather edge and the centre line. Firstly mark the centre line by setting the groover to ¾in (19mm), then mark the outer lines by setting the groover to ⅜in (10mm).

Firstly, stitch the furnishings into place (in this example we have used rings), then fold the leather and stitch. The stitching should start and end at the last stitches on the end of the returns. The stitches must be pulled up tight so that there is no gap visible between the two edges of the leather. It is important when stitching to ensure that the awl goes through the leather at right angles – otherwise the rolled area could twist; also, make sure that it comes out in the groove line on the back of the work piece.

The rolled area can be dampened to make it easier to fold and pull together when stitched. However, greater care must be taken as in this condition the leather is more prone to damage, and the wet leather tends to grip the awl blades making stitching more difficult.

Once the stitching is complete, trim off any excess. Then use the skiver to reduce the distance between the stitch line and the edge of the leather to approximately a ⅟₁₆in (1.25mm) taking great care not to take off too much or cut the stitching. Keep checking both sides of the edges as it is easy to reduce one side more than the other. Again, taking care not to cut the stitches, run a No. 4 edge shave along both sides, then edge dye. Finally, place the rolled area into a rolling block and tap it into shape. Finish in the normal manner.

Rolled handle dimensions.

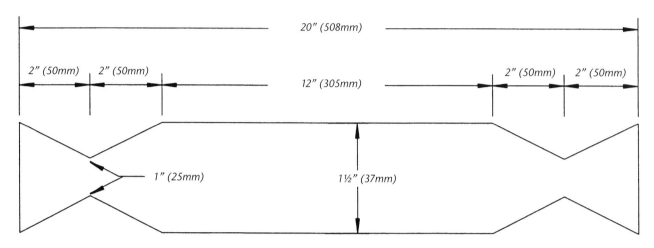

20" (508mm)

2" (50mm)   2" (50mm)   12" (305mm)   2" (50mm)   2" (50mm)

1" (25mm)   1½" (37mm)

·– – – – – – – – = Stitch marking

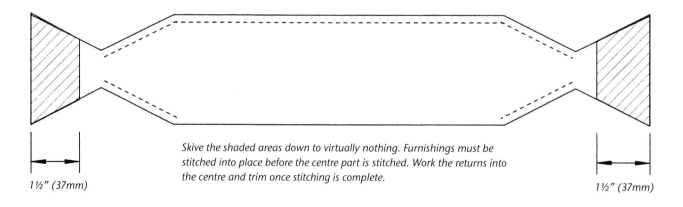

Skive the shaded areas down to virtually nothing. Furnishings must be stitched into place before the centre part is stitched. Work the returns into the centre and trim once stitching is complete.

1½" (37mm)   1½" (37mm)

MAKING A ROLLED HANDLE

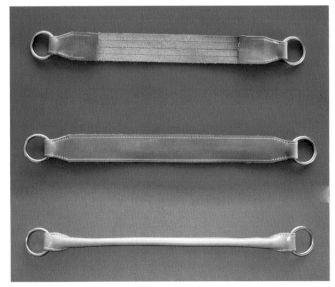

(top) Groove lines placed on flesh side to aid rolling; *(middle)* rings stitched into place first; *(bottom)* completed item.

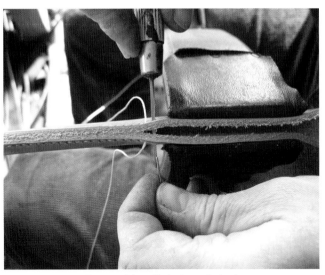

Centre of handle being stitched.

Trimming off the excess.

Shaping in the rolling block.

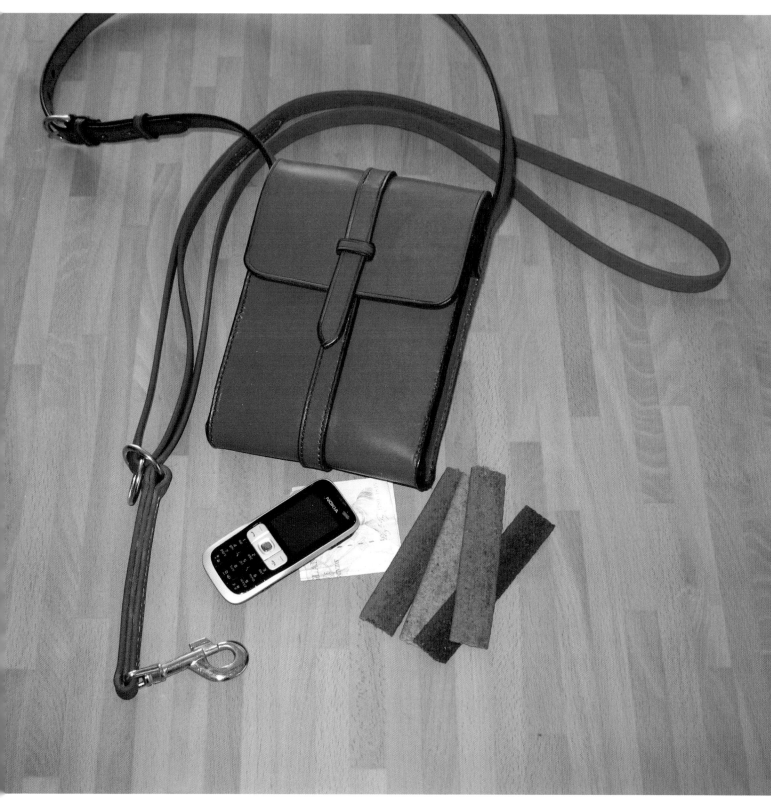

A small shoulder bag.

CHAPTER 5

DESIGN AND PATTERNS

Design

The idea and design of all items is born from a 'need' or 'want'. An example of this is women's handbags: there was a need for women to have somewhere to carry personal belongings so the idea of the handbag was developed. Women then wanted more eye-catching designs so over the years makers competed to produce them. It is unlikely that the majority of us will ever design an item that is entirely new. It is more likely that we see something and alter its construction to fit our requirements. Look around the shops and in magazines and catalogues for inspiration.

Don't be put off by the complexity of an item; it always looks much simpler once broken down into its component parts. Experienced leatherworkers can have problems getting a new design right first time so don't be disheartened (workshops around the country are full of items that have gone wrong). Be adaptable; stop and think about any problems that may arise, then work around them. It can't be stressed enough – enjoy yourself. So your first attempt has come out looking clumsy. Most importantly you took on a project that was difficult for you, and you made it the best you could at the time. Providing that you know what's been done wrong, next time it will be better.

Planning

Planning is the key to the successful outcome of a project. Keeping a pattern book will prove very useful for recording the information about your projects along with other useful information such as costing. This not only allows you to easily remake a project but can also serve as a reminder as to where

problems may have been encountered and/or solutions to these problems. At the end of a project, note any suggestions as to how the project could be improved if remade in the future. Label each project clearly and make sure that any corresponding patterns cut for the project are labelled with the same name.

Stage 1: Initial Plans

This is the most important stage. Consider the finished item. What is its purpose and how is it going to look? A bag that is faultless in its manufacture is not much use if it will only carry A5 size documents when all your documents are A4.

Sit down and sketch your idea onto paper taking into consideration the following points:

- The simpler the design the easier it will be to construct.
- Smooth curved lines are sometimes more pleasing to the eye than sharp angles (and are often easier to construct).

Stage 2: Breakdown

Break the item down into its component parts. Take the belt pouch made in the previous chapter as an example. It has three component parts: front piece; back piece and belt loop. Draw each individual piece, including the dimensions for each. If gussets are required the width can be decided on at this point, but calculate the length after the cutting patterns have been made.

Next consider what furnishings will be required, items like buckles, fastenings etc. How and where will these items be attached? Any attachments should be marked in the relevant position on the drawings. What type of leather is to be used? If the project is to be dyed, what colour is required?

Stage 3: Construction Plan

Again using the belt pouch as an example, imagine that you have designed it, cut out all the pieces, then moulded and laced the front and back pieces together – but you are left with the belt loop. The whole piece would then have to be taken apart, because there is no way to stitch it into place once the pouch is made up. When pieces start to take shape, in the excitement it is very easy to overlook the little pieces.

Examine the drawings and establish the easiest method of construction, then write a sequence of events list. For the belt pouch it would be as follows:

1. Prepare the pieces.
2. Dye, then fix the press stud.
3. Stitch the belt loop to the back piece.
4. Mould and lace front and back pieces together.

As can be seen there is no need to list things like 'cut the leather' as this should be fairly obvious. Often the construction plan is finalized once the cutting patterns are made. The final stage is to make the patterns.

Pattern Making

There is no need to make patterns for simple projects like a belt or for pieces like a straight gusset; merely make a note of the dimensions. With more complex projects the making of patterns can highlight problems before the leather is cut, thus reducing wastage.

Before embarking on the intricacies of pattern making, it is worth reiterating the difference between cut size and made-up size and how they relate to patterns. These terms apply to any project regardless of whether or not patterns are made.

Made-up size is the actual size that the item will be when assembled. The paper patterns made in the initial stages conform to the made-up sizes.

Cut size is the actual size that the leather is cut to, calculated by adding any allowances to the made-up sizes. The cutting patterns conform to the cut sizes.

Initial Stages

Initially draw each component part of the project onto plain paper; do not include any seam or turning allowances. Then cut them out. These patterns are used as working patterns to confirm shapes and sizes.

When drawing a shape where two opposite sides need to be symmetrical, fold the paper in half, draw one half of the shape on the folded paper, then cut it out. When making patterns for items that consist of front and back pieces, and part or the entire back piece needs to be identical to the front piece, make the pattern for the front first, then use it to form the matching part of the back piece. This ensures they will be identical when joined.

Inspect the patterns closely; pieces always look different once viewed in their full form. Adjust as necessary, i.e. you may decide that a shallower curve on the side would look better. There is a great temptation, especially when making a bag, to keep adding a bit on – the end result being that the item is too big to be practical. At this stage it sometimes helps to make a copy of the patterns, then to assemble one copy using tape. This will give a better overall view of the project once assembled.

Cutting Patterns

These are the patterns that will be used to mark and cut the leather. Following the outline of a paper pattern is very difficult as the edges tend to move, so use a thick card. Mounting board is ideal, and for smaller projects, cereal packets will suffice. The edges of the card tend to be worn away with use so patterns that are in constant use are better made from $1/8$in (3mm) thick MDF board. This can be cut using a Stanley knife, and as with leather, marking it with a scratch awl will help to guide the blade.

Remember, if the patterns are not correct the end project will be wrong, so it is worth spending time getting them as accurate as possible. A fine grade of sandpaper can be used on MDF or card to tidy the edges.

Transfer the paper patterns to the card. Then set a pair of compasses to the desired allowances and carefully trace around the outline where the allowances are required (weights placed on the patterns will hold them in place). Then cut out the patterns (including the allowances) and tidy as necessary. Cutting thick card with scissors can be difficult, and often using a clickers knife or Stanley knife is the better option.

Where two pieces are to be joined, place a few Vs at strategic points and transfer these to the corresponding pattern. These are used to position the two pieces of leather when joined, to ensure they go together square. To calculate the length of gussets, place a piece of string or thread around the outline of the gusseted piece. Remove the string and measure it against a ruler. Note the length and the position of any Vs.

Pattern Markings

The position of furnishings, and where stitching runs are to start and end, need to be marked. Place a small hole in these positions and label each clearly. When marking the position of fastenings such as press studs, to ensure a correct fit only mark the position of one of the parts and then position the other part once the project is assembled. This position can be recorded for future use.

Example

If this was the first time the belt pouch was assembled the position of the press stud on the flap would not be marked. After assembly the flap is folded to the closed position and pressed firmly against the male part of the press stud. (The male part of the press stud is positioned first because it would be difficult to fix it in place once the pouch was assembled). An impression of the stud will be made on the flesh side of the flap which can be used to position the female part of the stud. If you have difficulty seeing the impression, rub a pencil over the stud; the graphite will be transferred giving a better impression.

Many patterns will have every conceivable instruction written on them. This can be confusing, and instructions can easily be missed. It is better to keep instructions written on the pattern to a minimum, and to record additional information in the pattern book instead.

Making Moulded Pouch Patterns

These types of patterns are a bit more involved but with a little thought should not be beyond the scope of the beginner. As the basic shape of these items is a rectangle there is probably no need to make paper patterns but if you are more comfortable making them, then go ahead.

Regardless of size, all these items will have two or three components; back piece, front piece and belt loop, if includ-

POSITIONING THE PRESS STUD

Rub a pencil over the male part of the stud and press the flap firmly onto it.

A graphite mark will be transferred onto the flap (the mark has been exaggerated for clarity).

ed. The important thing to remember when making these patterns is that the width of the base on the front and back pieces need to be the same.

The made up sizes relate to the front piece and are thought of in terms of length, width and depth. As an example let us assume that we want to make a pouch 4in (101mm) long by 3in (76mm) wide by 1in (25mm) deep.

ALLOWANCES

We need to allow for the stitched edges to be folded out so that they are flat against the back piece when stitched. On most natural vegetable tanned leathers, an allowance of ¼in (6mm) will be sufficient. This allowance is made up from $\frac{1}{8}$in (3mm) stitching allowance and $\frac{1}{8}$in (3mm) for the fold. On very heavy and pre-dyed leathers this may require increasing.

CUT SIZES

When calculating the widths remember there are two sides (left and right) so allowances and depth, if appropriate, will need to be added twice. On the length it is added once (to form the bottom part) as the top either forms the flap or is open.

Back Piece Cut Width = Made-up Width + (Allowance x2)

Back Piece Cut Length = (Made-up Length × 1.5) + Depth + Allowance + ½in (12mm) – the first two parts of the equation allow enough room for the flap to fold over the top of the front piece and finish halfway down. The ½in (12mm) is to allow for the thickness of the leather as it folds over the top.

Front Piece Cut Width = Made-up Width + (Made-up Depth × 2) + (Allowance × 2)

Cut Length = Made-up Length + Allowance – Do not add the depth to the length, as the base will be tapered to the same width on the back piece.

Using our example we would have a front piece of 4¼in (107mm) long by 5½in (139mm) wide and a back piece of 7¾in (197mm) long by 3½in (88mm) wide. Draw two rectangles to the dimensions; use a pencil as they will require altering. Draw a centre line down the length of both pieces.

BACK PIECE

Round the bottom two corners using an appropriately sized coin. Then measure 5¾in (146mm) from the bottom and place a mark on either side. From these marks shape the end of the flap to a design of your choosing. This measurement is calculated using the formula: Made-up Length + Allowance + Depth + ½in (12mm). This gives an allowance for the flap to fold over the top of the front piece before shaping.

Take the length of the front piece and reduce it by $\frac{1}{8}$in (3mm). Using this size, measure from the bottom of the piece and place a mark on either of the outside edges. This indicates where the stitch holes will start and finish if the item is to be laced together.

FRONT PIECE

This piece requires tapering so that the width of the base matches the width of the back piece. From the centre line, mark the width of the back piece onto the bottom edge; make sure they are of equal proportions either side of the line. On the outside edges, place marks at the halfway point, then connect these marks to the base marks; this forms the taper. Once cut out, use a fine grade piece of sandpaper to round the shoulder. This distance can be reduced for shallower depths of pouch. Use the back piece as a pattern to round the bottom corners; place Vs in the corresponding corners of both pieces; these indicate where to join the pieces.

Mark the position of the fastening, which will depend on the type of fastening being used. If you remember that the flap will come halfway down the length of the front piece, this will give you the amount of room to play with. In this example we have 2in (50mm) to play with (front cut size divided by 2). If a press stud is to be used, a good distance would be 1in (25mm) from the top edge. This will leave enough room for the female part of the stud to be fixed to the flap without being too close to the leather edge. The position of the stud on the back piece is determined after one of these pouches has been made.

The width and length of the belt loop will depend on the pouch size and is best left until the assembly process. The best method is to cut a strip of leather to the desired width leaving it long; then measure it against the back piece to get the required length. Record these dimensions for future use.

Making Formers

Formers are used for the moulding of leather and can be made from any material that will not compress under pressure. On projects like the belt pouch these items do not have to be a work of art providing they give the required shape. However on large projects like shotgun cases they are used as part of the pattern and must be exactly right. MDF board and wood are ideal materials. Plastozote (high density foam easily shaped with a Stanley knife or Surform and impervious to water) can be used on smaller projects.

To make a former is straightforward. Stick layers of wood or MDF board together to achieve the correct depth; mark the required shape onto the surface and cut it out. However, born from experience there are a few little tips worth noting:

▦ When wet, leather can be stretched but then shrinks back when drying, tending to grip the former. It is not unheard of for formers to be stuck so tightly that it necessitates the dismantling of the project to release it. Smoothing the surfaces, rounding the edges and tapering the end of the former slightly will help alleviate this problem.
▦ Wood will absorb water, which could cause it to swell; a few coats of wood sealer will prevent this.
▦ On large projects coat the former with a leather feed. Since most leather feeds are slightly greasy to the touch this lubricates the former.
▦ Ensure that provision is made for removing formers that will be totally encased by the leather, such as drilling a hole in the end enabling a screw to be inserted.
▦ Formers made for pouch type items should be at least 1in (25mm) longer than the made-up length to allow a good grip when being removed.
▦ Wet leather marks and damages easier than dry leather. Any sharp angles on the former should be rounded off to prevent damage when being inserted.
▦ The dimensions should be $\frac{1}{8}$in (3mm) less all round than the made-up size.
▦ Formers prevent the circulation of air around the inside of the project, which could cause mildew to form. Removing the former in the latter stages of drying will prevent this.

MAKING PATTERNS FROM FORMERS

It is possible to take a pattern for the front piece of a moulded project directly from a former. This technique is an ideal way of obtaining the basic shape of the front piece of a moulded item.

TAKING PATTERNS FROM A FORMER

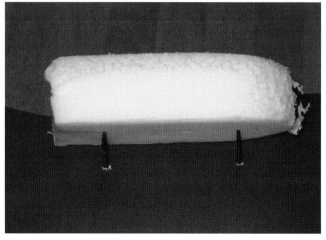

Securing the former by pinning it to a piece of card from the underneath.

Going over the outline with a pattern marker.

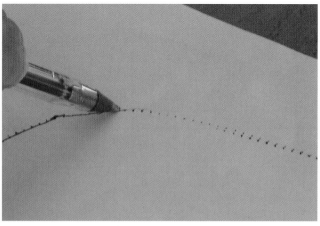

Tracing the outline of the marks left by the pattern marker.

The former needs to be secured so that it cannot move. The best method is to pin the former to a piece of thick card from the underneath (i.e. pin through the card into the former).

Using tailor's chalk, draw a straight line on a piece of cloth. Place the cloth over the former – the line should be placed in the centre of the former. Pull the cloth tight ensuring that no creases are present. Keep the cloth in place by pinning it to the former and at strategic points around it. When tracing the outline on one side of the former it is possible that the cloth on the opposite side will be pulled up. Therefore, the pins should be placed in a manner to prevent this from happening. Push the cloth into the join between the former and card and trace the outline using the chalk. Trace over the top of the former, coming up the one side, over the top and down the other side. The former may be longer than the actual length of the front piece, so remember to adjust the outline accordingly; the tracing over the top should be at the actual length of the front piece, not the length of the former.

Fold a piece of paper in half, then lay it out so that the crease line is visible. Remove the cloth and chalk a line down the centre of the resultant outline. Lay the cloth on the paper, lining up the centre line with the crease; it is important to get this as accurate as possible. Go over the outline with a pattern marker (a pattern marker is similar to a stitching wheel except that the points are narrower and sharper). If a pattern marker is not available, go along the outline with a scratch awl, stabbing through the cloth at close intervals. When the cloth is removed the outline should be defined by a series of small holes.

Go over the outline with a pencil, tidying any uneven lines. The two sides will probably not be symmetrical, so fold the paper along the crease and work on the side that has the better shape. Remember, the former has been made $\frac{1}{8}$in (3mm) smaller all round than the made-up size; therefore check and adjust the sizes as necessary. This now gives us a working pattern that can be made into a cutting pattern.

PRACTICE PROJECT

Small Shoulder Bag

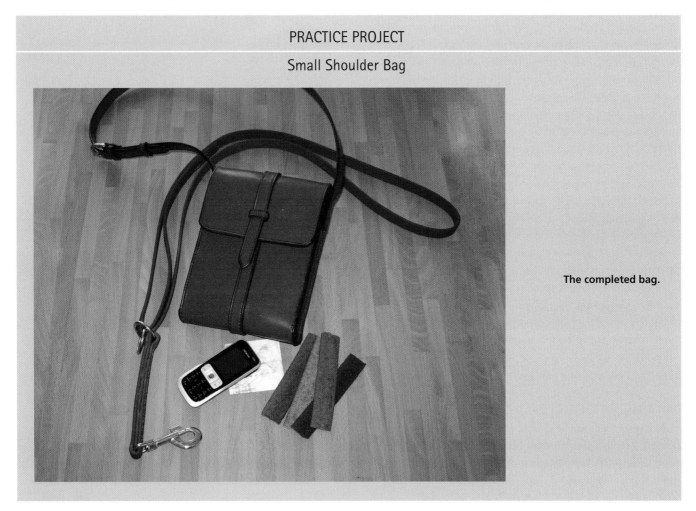

The completed bag.

PRACTICE PROJECT: Small Shoulder Bag *continued*

Here we are going to put into practice the principles of design and pattern making by taking a project from its conception to construction.

PLANNING

Sitting amidst a pile of discarded plans we arrive at a design that we are happy with. A simple bag made from a single piece of leather wrapped around two side gussets. The dimensions decided on are 8in (203mm) long, 6in (152mm) wide and 1in (25mm) deep. Stitched to the centre of the bag will be a ¾in (19mm) lay (a strip of leather stitched to the main piece), which will be used to form a strap and loop fastening.

A strap and loop fastening is simply a loop of leather stitched into place in the same manner as a fixed keeper. A hole is then cut into the flap slightly larger than the loop. When closed the loop will jut out through this hole, and a strap of leather is then pushed through it, thus securing the flap.

The shoulder strap will also be ¾in (19mm), made in two parts with a buckle to allow for adjustment. We have decided to use a 2–2.5mm vegetable tanned shoulder pre-dyed red.

Broken down into its component parts the bag consists of:

- A main piece
- Two side gussets
- Centre lay and loop
- Two-part shoulder strap
- Furnishings: one ¾in (19mm) buckle

Our construction plan would be:

1. Cut and prepare pieces
2. Stitch lay and loop to main piece
3. Stitch buckle to shoulder strap
4. Stitch shoulder strap to gussets (it would be possible to stitch the shoulder straps once the bag has been constructed, but it would prove quite awkward)
5. Stitch gussets to main piece

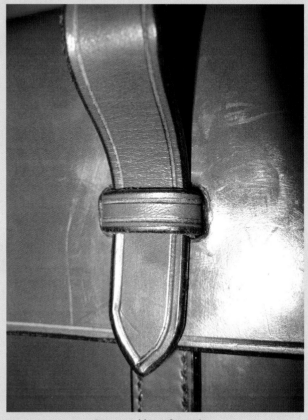

Strap and loop fastening.

PATTERNS

Next the working patterns require drawing and cutting. In reality, for a project this simple where the basic shapes are rectangles and strips of leather, there is no need to make patterns. However, if you are unsure of how the finished item will look, always make the patterns (*see* overleaf).

At this point we are unsure of how much overlap to leave on the flap, how long the centre lay needs to be, where to position the loop, how long to make the shoulder strap and how much stitching will be required on the lay. By making two sets of working patterns and making one up using tape, we can calculate and record these lengths. Add 1½in (37mm) to the buckle part of the shoulder strap to accommodate the buckle return.

The loop needs to be long enough to protrude through the flap when closed, leaving enough space for

PRACTICE PROJECT: Small Shoulder Bag *continued*

Shoulder bag: cut dimensions.

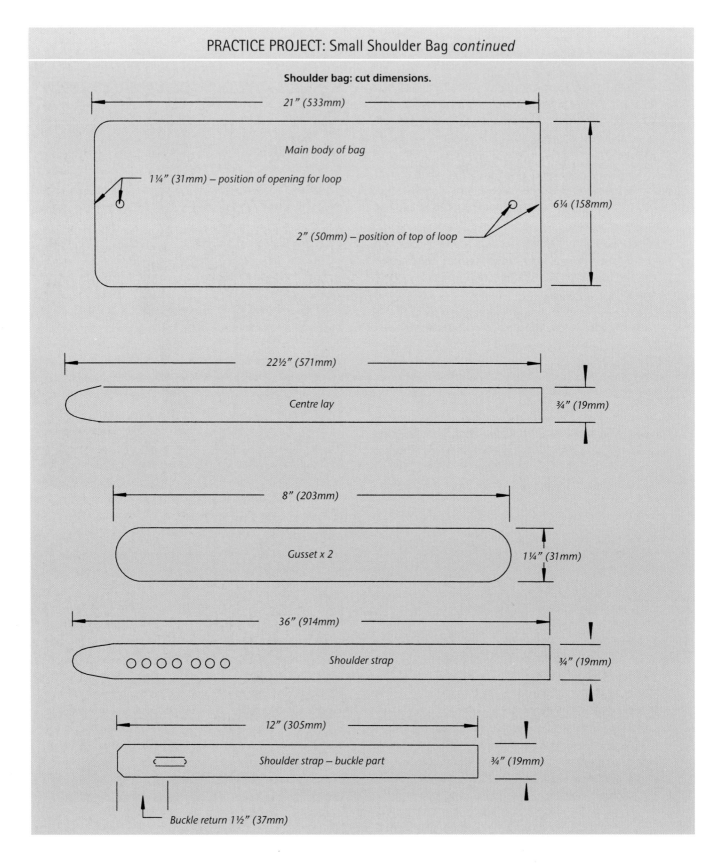

21" (533mm)

Main body of bag

1¼" (31mm) – position of opening for loop

2" (50mm) – position of top of loop

6¼ (158mm)

22½" (571mm)

Centre lay

¾" (19mm)

8" (203mm)

Gusset x 2

1¼" (31mm)

36" (914mm)

Shoulder strap

¾" (19mm)

12" (305mm)

Shoulder strap – buckle part

¾" (19mm)

Buckle return 1½" (37mm)

PRACTICE PROJECT: Small Shoulder Bag *continued*

the end of the lay to pass through it. A square will need to be cut out of the flap to house the loop (this best left until the bag is constructed so that an accurate position can be established).

The working patterns are now transferred to thick card and the allowances added. We have decided to allow ¹/₈in (3mm) for stitching. This is now added to the main piece and gussets on the cutting patterns. To mark the position of the loop, make a hole in the pattern. When the patterns are transferred to the leather a scratch awl can be pushed through this hole to make a small 'dot' on the leather. Finally the positions where the gussets are to join to the main piece require marking.

Marking Vs (Joining Marks)

As already discussed, the Vs must line up exactly on all corresponding pieces. The best method to employ on this project is to mark the gussets first, then transfer them to the main piece. All sides of the gussets will require stitching, with the exception of the top opening. Therefore the stitching will start and end at the top of the gusset, and the marks indicating this should be exactly opposite each other.

1. Place a V at the start and end of the stitching and at the bottom of the gusset.
2. Place a V on the top end of main piece (the end opposite the flap closure). This is where the stitching will start.
3. Using a piece of thread or string, lay it along the edge of the gusset, beginning where the V which denotes the start stitching has been placed. Place a mark on the thread corresponding to the V on the bottom of the gusset.
4. Transfer this measurement to the main piece. Starting at the V that indicates the start of the stitching, lay the thread along the edge of the main piece and place a V at the point where the thread has been marked.
5. Repeat points 3 and 4, working from the V on the bottom of the gusset to the V at the end of the stitching. Once transferred, the last V will also denote the end of the stitching on the main piece.

ASSEMBLY

Preparation

Using the cutting patterns, mark and cut out all the required pieces of leather including the centre lay, shoulder straps and looping. Cut the looping to ³/₈in (10mm) wide. Make sure that all joining and placement points are transferred to the pieces. Place a groove line ¹/₈in (3mm) from the edge around all the pieces. Using a No. 2 edge shave, edge shave the pieces in accordance with the illustration. Then dye the edges and groove lines. Using a 7 per inch (25mm) stitch marker, place the stitch marks as illustrated.

The shoulder strap has seven holes starting 2in (50mm) from the end spaced 1in (25mm) apart. The length of the strap and number of holes may be adjusted to suit your own requirements.

A better join is made if the edges of the gussets and the parts of the main piece that they are to be stitched to are shaved to a 45 degree angle. An easy method of obtaining this angle is to set the dividers to the thickness of the leather, then draw a line on the flesh side along the areas to be stitched. Taking great care not to cut into the actual piece, skive the edge as shown in the illustration, using a skiver or skirt shave. It is important that any stitch marking is performed before creating the 45 degree angle.

Creating a 45 degree angle using the skirt shave.

PRACTICE PROJECT: Small Shoulder Bag *continued*

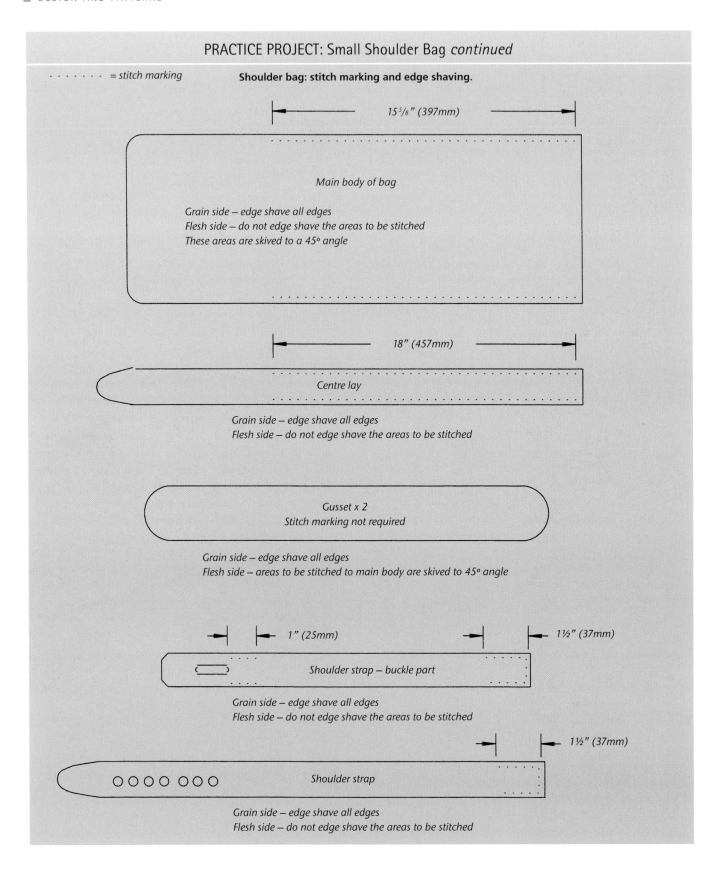

· · · · · · · = *stitch marking*   **Shoulder bag: stitch marking and edge shaving.**

15⁵/₈" (397mm)

Main body of bag

Grain side – edge shave all edges
Flesh side – do not edge shave the areas to be stitched
These areas are skived to a 45° angle

18" (457mm)

Centre lay

Grain side – edge shave all edges
Flesh side – do not edge shave the areas to be stitched

Gusset x 2
Stitch marking not required

Grain side – edge shave all edges
Flesh side – areas to be stitched to main body are skived to 45° angle

1" (25mm)   1½" (37mm)

Shoulder strap – buckle part

Grain side – edge shave all edges
Flesh side – do not edge shave the areas to be stitched

1½" (37mm)

Shoulder strap

Grain side – edge shave all edges
Flesh side – do not edge shave the areas to be stitched

Gussets tack stitched in place ready for stitching.

Construction

All the stitching should be done using a saddle stitch and an 18/4 thread.

1. Position the lay in the centre of the main piece and pin into place. Position the loop, and stitch the lay into place. The loop is treated in the same manner as a fixed keeper and should be blocked up once the lay has been stitched into position.
2. Stitch the buckle onto the shoulder strap. Depending on the type of buckle used, a fixed keeper may be required. However, always make and fit a running keeper.
3. Stitch the shoulder strap to the gussets. Make sure that any keepers are blocked up before performing this task.

4. Tack stitch one of the gussets to the main piece, ensuring that the joining Vs are lined up. Stitch the gusset into place. Then repeat the process with the remaining gusset.
5. Fold the flap into place and mark the position of the loop. Carefully cut out a square approximately $1/16$in (1.5mm) larger than the loop all round. Dye the edges of the resultant hole.

Finishing

Re-dye and polish the joins where the gussets have been stitched to the main piece, using a polishing bone. The edges should look like a single piece with no visible join. Feed and polish the whole item using a good leather feed.

A variety of stamps, stencils and designs used for carving and stamping leather.

CHAPTER 6

DECORATION

Leather can be decorated in many ways, from simply raising the centre of a belt to more elaborate methods such as carving, stamping and colouring. Purpose made studs, emblems and even rivets with decorative heads can also be purchased for the use of decoration. In fact, with a little ingenuity and artistic flair the possibilities are endless. A word of warning: as with everything, decoration requires practice and attention to detail. It is very easy to get carried away, leaving an item looking garish. Think out your designs carefully.

Carving and Stamping

The techniques described here are written for use with stamping and carving tools, but effective designs can also be made using the groover and creases.

Carving and stamping are only suitable for use on full grain vegetable tanned leathers, as they will absorb water which is essential to achieve a good impression on the leather surface. The grain of the leather is necessary to allow the leather to hold the shape when dry.

Stamping is best performed on a smooth hard surface such as a piece of polished marble or granite. Both are readily available at leathercraft suppliers. This also applies to carving as it is normally combined with stamping.

These are great activities to get the children involved with. The only sharp tool involved is the swivel knife when carving, and obviously supervision will be required when this is employed.

Casing Leather

Casing is the term used for preparing the leather prior to carving or stamping. This loosens the leather fibres which in turn soften the surface, making it more receptive to the stamping or carving processes. Try stamping or carving a piece of dry scrap leather; then try it on a damp piece and you will see the need for casing.

The term 'casing' is believed to derive from when the leather would be soaked until it no longer floated on the water; it would then be wrapped in a woollen blanket (encased) to exclude the air and raise the humidity, and left for twelve hours. The leather would then be taken out and left grain side upmost to dry to the correct consistency. This technique is still employed in our workshop (and probably in many others) when working on larger projects or heavy leathers, as we consider it to be the best method of preparing the leather to achieve the best results. However, many prefer a quicker method of casing.

Use sponge or a flower spray to dampen first the flesh side of the leather, then the grain side, ensuring that the surfaces are evenly covered. The leather will darken as the water penetrates the surface. If the leather dries out almost immediately (starts to return to its normal colour) add more water. As a guide, leave the leather for a few seconds, then hold it against your cheek; if it feels warm then it is too dry; if it feels cool then it is damp and ready to be used. When the leather has almost returned to its original colour, it is ready to carve. On large projects the leather may dry out and require further dampening. It only takes a little practice to become accustomed to how the correct texture of the surface should feel.

Working cased leather requires a little care and attention. The surface will mark and pick up dirt very easily, and these can be very difficult if not impossible to remove. Keep the work surface clean. Do not allow tools to rest on the leather, as certain metals can stain the surface. This also applies to the water used for casing – do not put it in metal containers. Finally, wash your hands, as dirt from them could mark the surface.

If you need to leave the design before it is complete, put it in an airtight bag and place it in the fridge, which will prevent it from drying out and will delay the onset of mildew.

Stamping

Many think of stamping and embossing as the same, but they are two distinct processes. Embossing involves the use of a press and embossing plates to imprint the leather, while stamping involves the use of pre-made stamps that are struck. Leathercraft shops have vast arrays of stamps in many shapes and sizes. These also include letter and number stamps, ideal for making key rings with names and numbers. There are specific stamps that are used in conjunction with carving but can also be used singularly to produce geometrical designs.

When not used in conjunction with carving, stamping is a simple matter of dampening the leather surface, placing the stamp in the required position and striking it with a mallet. If stamping onto leather that is to be dyed, stamp after dyeing the leather, as it can sometimes be difficult to get the dye into the impression.

Carving

Carving is a method of creating a three-dimensional design by cutting and stamping the leather surface. The design is transferred onto the leather, and then the lines are carved with the swivel knife. Stamping tools such as bevellers or pear shaders are then used to create the effect.

The beauty of carving is that even the learning process is great fun and very therapeutic. Although there are basic techniques to master, it lends itself to individual styles, and practised leatherworkers never stop learning new aspects whenever a new project is attempted.

TRANSFER PATTERNS

A transfer pattern is a drawing of the outline of a design indicating the lines to be cut with the swivel knife. These are normally traced, but you can also scan the design into a computer and print it onto acetate (clear film used with overhead projectors). This method can pose problems for the beginner, as decisions such as which lines to include will have to be made while the design is being transferred onto the leather.

Designs can be obtained by simply tracing a picture from magazines, books, etc or bought as a stencil from leathercraft suppliers. These are made from plastic with one side raised to conform to the design. This side is placed onto cased leather, and the back is firmly rubbed with a blunt instrument such as an awl handle. Stencils will also come with a picture of the completed design which is used to create the carving.

As any tracings will be placed onto damp leather it is better to use tracing film. This has a glossy side which goes against the leather and is waterproof, and a matte side onto which the tracing is made. Initially, do not be too ambitious, start with simple designs. Do a simple design reasonably well and you will be encouraged; do a complicated design that ends in disaster and you are more likely to give up.

Tracing

Tracing is generally thought of as a simple matter of placing the tracing paper on the chosen design and tracing it. However if the process of tracing is done using the following method it aids the decision making in the creation stages. Study the design carefully and try to envisage it in layers; the areas that are in the foreground first, then the areas behind this and so on. To explain this more clearly think of the numbers 1 to 4 lined up on a table, one behind the other, in ascending numerical order. No. 1 is the closest to you, the foreground; No. 2 the next closest, down to No. 4, the background. This is the order that the design should be traced, from foreground to background, completing each layer before moving on to the next. Tracing each layer in a different colour will serve as a reminder as to which is which. To ensure that the tracing film does not move, use paper clips or masking tape to hold it in position. Make sure that the glossy side is on the design and that you are drawing on the matte side.

Transferring the Tracing

The leather must be cased, and any borders encapsulating the design must be marked using the dividers, before the design is transferred. Place the tracing over the leather (glossy side

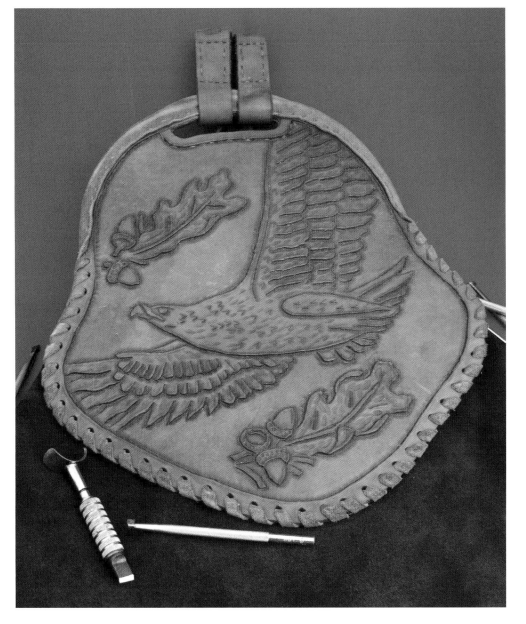

Design used to decorate a bag.

on the leather) and in the centre of the borderlines, if any; use masking tape to secure the film in place. Then use a tracing stylus or any dull pointed instrument to carefully re-trace the lines in the same order that they were traced – foreground to background. Press firmly but not too hard, as there is a danger of ripping through the film. The lines will be indented onto the leather surface. Before removing the tracing, carefully lift one corner to ensure that all the lines have been re-traced. The design is then cut in the order it was traced.

One of the most difficult task beginners have is deciding where to shade, where to bevel etc. Tracing, transferring and cutting each layer in the same order helps to build up a picture of how each layer sits within the design, which in turn makes these decisions much easier.

SWIVEL KNIFE

This is used to make the bold cuts that define the outline of the pattern. The knife is made up of three parts: the yoke, the barrel and the blade. Depending on the type of knife purchased the yoke will be either fixed, or adjustable to suit the size of your hand.

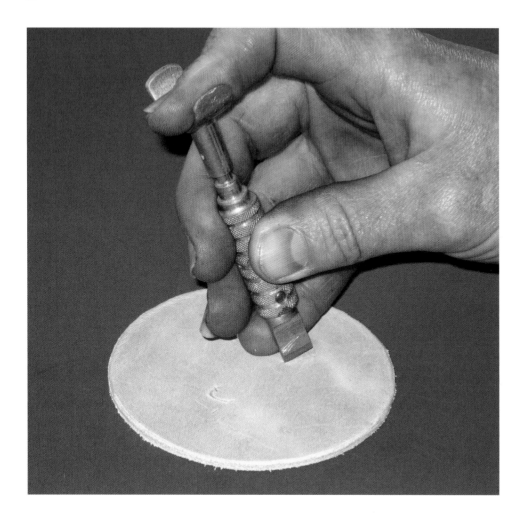

Holding the swivel knife on the leather.

The blades are interchangeable and are held in the barrel by means of a small screw. Regular blades come in width sizes of ½in (12mm), ³⁄₈in (10mm) and ¼in (6mm). Also available are *angled blades* which are slightly angled; *filigree blades* which have a sharper angle and are used for cutting background areas and fine details; and *hair blades* which are used to draw hair on animals.

As with any knife, it is important that these are kept sharp to obtain a clean precise cut, and on large projects they may need constant stropping. Although sharpening and stropping are performed in the same manner as with any other knife, it is very important that the cutting edge is central and even on both sides.

Usage

The swivel knife is designed to twist and turn as it cuts, and it is surprisingly sensitive. Spend a little time familiarizing yourself with the knife and practising cuts. The knife is held with the index/first finger resting on the yoke (this controls the depth of cut depending on the pressure placed upon it) and the second and third fingers gripping the barrel (these control the movement of the knife). Resting the little finger on the leather beside the blade helps with control of the blade. The important thing is that the knife feels comfortable in the hand. If your grip varies from that described, providing it allows the knife to be used in the correct manner, then carry on.

Case the leather. Then holding the knife as described, place the knife upright on the leather so that it is at 90 degrees to the surface. (It is important to maintain this position while cutting as any deviation will result in a condition known as *undercutting*, which looks unsightly and makes the later stages more difficult.) The cutting is done with the corner of the blade, so tilt the knife slightly forwards (away from you) and draw it towards you.

Swivel knife cutting exercises.

Small arrows indicated the directions of the cuts

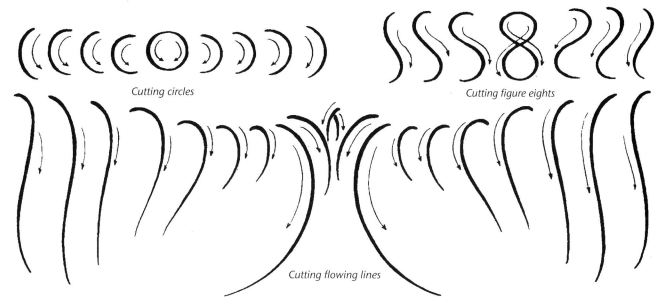

Cutting circles

Cutting figure eights

Cutting flowing lines

Make cuts with one long flowing motion. Turn leather when necessary to aid smooth cutting

Make cutting strokes towards your body for maximum control. Do not double-cut any of the lines

Cutting Exercises

The key to successful cutting is to relax. Many will try too hard and tense up which makes control difficult, if not impossible, and also makes your arm ache. Sit comfortably in a well lit area with a firm grip on the knife but not trying to throttle the life out of it!

Practise the exercises on scrap leather. Remember to case the leather first. The depth of the cut should be approximately half the thickness of the leather and should be constant throughout. Make the cuts in one flowing movement; stopping will result in ragged lines. As the cut sweeps around a curve, use the free hand to manoeuvre the leather so that the knife is always drawn towards you, which gives maximum control. Do not try to re-cut lines as it is very difficult to accurately follow a previously cut line. More often than not, the lines are left with double cuts. Always keep the knife upright.

Decorative Cuts

Decorative cuts are normally made after all carving and stamping but before the back grounding. They are used to enhance the project. However, bad decorative cuts can ruin a project, so if you are not confident in your ability it is best to leave them out.

The cut itself should flow with the natural curves of the design and should be as graceful as possible. Place the knife on the leather with the blade pointing to the 10 o'clock position. Start with a heavy downward pressure, and as soon as the cut is started begin to make the turn. As the cut starts to straighten, gradually reduce the pressure so that it fades to nothing at the end.

STAMPING TOOLS

The stamping tools used in carving are designed to produce specific effects to build up a design. As there are numerous stamping tools available, only the most commonly used have been described. Other stamping tools can be purchased and experimented with as you become more experienced. They can be used in many combinations, enabling your creative tendencies to run wild. Each basic tool is available with variations in size, serration pattern, curve and slope.

Holding and 'Walking' Tools

Most of these tools are used to fill in areas and require moving from one position to another; this is known as 'walking'. When struck, the force applied by the mallet should be even

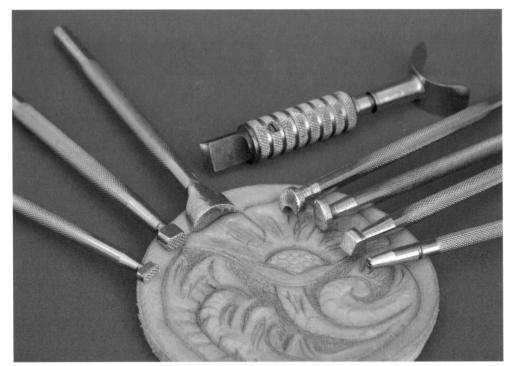

Tools used for carving leather: *(left to right)* small and large background tools, veiner, swivel knife, camouflage tool, pear shader, beveller, seeder.

Correct position to hold the stamping tools: Thumb below the centre of the shank with the fingers close together.

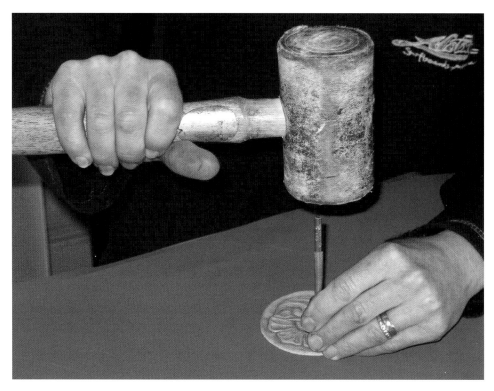

Correct way to hold the mallet when stamping.

to produce a uniform finish. Regardless of the type of tool being used they should all be 'walked' using the same method.

The tool should be held between the thumb and fingers, with the fingers close together and the thumb below the centre of the shank. The grip should be as light as possible but enough to stop the tool from flying out of your hand when stuck. Place the tool upright on the required position with the head just touching the surface of the leather. Rest the heel of the hand and little finger on the leather; the little finger should also be alongside the head of the tool and the hand relaxed. If the grip is right, when the tool is struck it will make the impression and bounce back to its original position ready to be moved to the next spot. (The tool is only moved approximately ¹/₁₆ in (1.5mm) between blows.) Taking advantage of the recoil not only saves effort but helps in the uniformity of the finish.

Mallets and Mauls

Mallets have already been discussed in Chapter 1; however, when stamping a carved design they are used in a different manner. A maul is basically a sideways-on mallet and comes in varying weights. As this form of stamping has many repetitive movements, if a lot of carving is envisaged, these are worth purchasing as they place less strain on the wrist. Both mallets and mauls are used in the same manner.

The stamping tool is normally held in the upright position when struck with the mallet. Unlike punching, these are more rhythmic taps rather than full struck blows. The handle of the mallet is held across the palm of the hand, being held with the fingers and resting on the thumb, not as it would be held for punching. Start by holding the handle in the centre; then adjust your grip to where the mallet feels comfortable and balanced. The wrist and the fingers act as a pivot for striking the tool. For most of the work the elbow will be resting on the bench, but when deeper impressions are required, adjust your grip towards the end of the handle and lift the elbow to exert more force.

Camouflage Tool

This tool has a half-moon shape with two sharp corners, known as the heels, while the wider curved end is the toe. The stamping surface has rounded serrations that normally fan out from a central focal point into a sunburst effect. This is used to texture particular areas of the design. By tilting the tool to the left or right, a heavy impression can be made on one side with the opposite side fading away to nothing. It can also be tipped forward onto the toe so that the heels do not dig in. When used in these positions, the tool needs to be held firmly to prevent it from slipping.

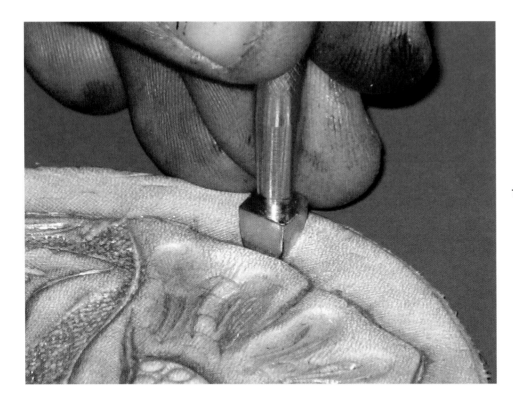

The beveller being walked along the cut lines.

Pear Shader

This tool shades or contours areas outlined by the swivel knife, producing a three-dimensional effect on the design by compressing and burnishing the leather to a darker contrasting colour. The stamping surface is rounded with no sharp edges; the wider end is the toe and the narrower end the heel. A smooth stamping surface is used in most applications, but slightly textured shaders are also available. Shading should follow the general shape of the design; in other words, study the original source of the design before deciding where to shade.

An artist will gradually diminish a colour to indicate changes in light and mood; this technique also applies when using the shader. The harder the tool is struck, the deeper the impression and the darker the colour. Start at the area that requires the deepest impression and 'walk' the shader towards the end. As the closing stages are reached, lessen the force of the blows so that the depressions become shallower, thus lightening the colour.

Practise shading until a smooth rhythmic action is achieved. Start slowly with a move–hit, move–hit movement and forget about speed; this will come naturally with practice. The shader can be 'walked' over very large areas and can be turned or tipped in the fingers between strokes to broaden or lessen the width of the shaded area and to control the direction of shading.

Beveller

The purpose of the beveller is to bring the design into bold relief by positioning it into the swivel cut and striking it. As with the pear shader, this action compresses and burnishes the leather. Usually only one side of the swivel knife cut is bevelled, but this is not a strict rule and will depend on the design. Some designs will require bevelling on alternate sides while others have it on both sides. There is also no set rule as to which side of the cut to bevel. An American saddle maker once told me that you should always bevel away from a stem (of a flower) and outside a curve; while this is a good adage for guidance it does not always apply. The original design will require studying, then a decision will be required as to which areas need to be brought into bold relief.

The beveller has a wedge shape with no sharp edges. The toe is the thicker end of the wedge; the flat surface running vertically to it (not the stamping surface) is the face; and the heel is the thinner end of the wedge. Hence the slope on the bevelling surface slopes from the toe to the heel. Although the most commonly used beveller has a smooth bevelling surface, they come in many sizes and textures for creating varied effects.

The toe of the beveller is always placed in the swivel cut with face towards the cut. 'Walk' the beveller in the same manner as the pear shader, turning the leather so that the face of the beveller is generally towards you. This gives you better visibility when working. Start with light taps of the mallet, increasing the force as you progress. At the end of the cut line, lessen the force of the blows, which has the effect of fading the bevel line in and out of the cut line. Unlike the pear shader the beveller should always be held upright and never tipped, which would allow the corners to dig into the leather leaving an uneven finish. As the beveller is 'walked', move the leather so that you are always working with the face of the beveller towards you.

Veiners

As the name implies, these are mainly used for adding veins to leaves, but they can be used for other decorative effects. A veiner is a curved tool with a scalloped inner edge and serrations on the stamping surface; it comes in many sizes.

The veiner is used in a similar way to the camouflage tool. It can be tipped left or right to increase the impression on one side and decrease the impression on the other. Depending on the degree the tool is leaned to one side, the width of the impression can be altered. When veining leaves, the impressions should be evenly spaced, gradually increasing in width as the leaf broadens.

Seeders

These are used to create the seed pods on flowers and have a small round stamping surface that is either smooth or textured. They are normally held upright on the leather, but if only a portion of the impression is required they can be tilted. The impressions should not overlap or be spaced too far apart. Start by stamping the outside rows first, then work towards the centre. A word of warning – as seeders have small round stamping surfaces, if struck too hard they can act like a punch and go right through the leather.

Backgrounds

The background tool is used to compress the background areas within and around the design. The stamping surface is stippled with teeth. They come in varying sizes and can be square or pear shaped. The most useful is the pear shaped as it has a small pointed end which can reach intricate areas. Never overlap into the actual design.

The tool is held upright and struck firmly with enough force to compress the leather to just below the cut line; all impressions should be uniform. It can be tilted towards the point to access the inaccessible areas. Over large areas the tool is 'walked' in the normal fashion, but as it is moved, turn the handle in the fingers to prevent a 'tooling pattern' from forming – i.e. if the shape of the stamping becomes visible it spoils the look of the pattern.

Stylus

A stylus, sometimes referred to as a modeller, is normally a double-ended tool with a point on one end and various shapes on the other end, the most common being a spoon or diamond shape. These are used for intricate work, and the pointed end (if rounded and dull) can be used to transfer traced patterns.

CARVING PROCEDURE

There is a set order in which each of the carving and stamping procedures is performed. This sequence is partly dictated by the moisture content of the leather, as individual stamping tools work better during each drying stage. The design will dictate which tools are required (i.e. if the design was a house it is unlikely you would use a veiner or seeder).

1. Transfer design
2. Carve outline
3. Camouflage tool
4. Pear shader
5. Beveller
6. Veiners
7. Seeders
8. Decorative cuts
9. Background tool

As the surface of the leather starts to dry but is still slightly dark, transfer the design and carve the outlines in the same order that they were traced. When it returns to its original colour, the surface will be firm and the inner fibres soft. This is when the best effects in burnishing and colour are achieved so this is the time to use the camouflage, shaders and bevellers. As the leather gets a little drier, the sharper tools – veiners and seeders – are used; then any decorative cuts may be added. Finally the leather surface will be firmer, which helps in achieving a smoother job of backgrounding.

PRACTICE PROJECT

Drinks Coaster

Transfer pattern for rounding.

Here we are going to practise the carving and stamping techniques discussed. We have placed our design onto a 3¼in (82mm) diameter circle of ⅛in (3mm) natural tanned leather which can be used as a drinks coaster.

Trace the design in the illustration: red line first (foreground), blue line second, followed by the green line (background). The black line circling the design indicates the size of the cut leather and does not require tracing. Cut and case the leather. Then transfer the design. Use the swivel knife to cut the outlines in the same order that they were traced.

Next use the camouflage tool to texture the stems and petals of the flower. Then use the pear shader to give the design more depth. Think as an artist would as to how the light would be represented on the design. Notice how shading over some of the camouflage impression tones down the impressions while still leaving a slight texture.

Bevel the outline. Then use the veiner to place the veins on the leaf. Next, use the seeder to create the seed pod. Then place the decorative cuts. If you are unsure of your ability on a real project it is best to leave these out, but remember, this is practice, so give it a try. The final stage is to use the background tool. Carved designs should be completed by using an antique finish or stain, which not only protects the design but also 'lifts' it, giving lustre and depth.

PRACTICE PROJECT

Drinks Coaster *continued*

(left) Design transferred onto the rounding; *(right)* Outline cut with swivel knife.

(left) Camouflaging; *(right)* Shading.

(left) Bevelling; *(right)* Veining.

PRACTICE PROJECT

Drinks Coaster *continued*

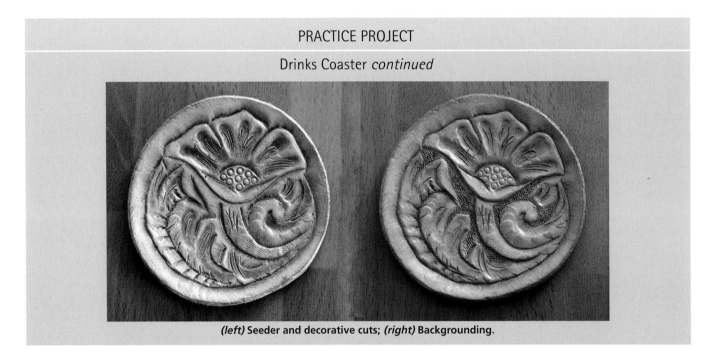

(left) Seeder and decorative cuts; *(right)* Backgrounding.

Studs and Ornaments

There are many types of studs and ornaments available, including domes, pyramids, horse's heads and shields, and they come in varying finishes and sizes. Methods of attaching these will vary: some have two prongs on the back that are pushed through the leather and bent over; some have a screw and thread arrangement; and others have a stud and cap rivet arrangement. In general studs should only be used on lined items as the lining hides the backs and gives a better finish. Studs with prongs should definitely only be used on lined items; otherwise the prongs could snag on other objects.

The size of stud, ornament, etc will depend on the project, but there must sufficient room around it to allow for the stitching.

Cut-Out and Inlaid Work

This type of work comes in a variety of forms. The simplest is where shapes are cut out of one piece of leather and joined to another, often using contrasting colours. The shapes do not have to be complicated: a simple arrangement of punched holes can prove very effective. Other methods will involve weaving lacing between pre-cut slits, placing fillets to raise softer leather through the cut-out or simply stitching fancy patterns.

We have used belts to describe the following techniques as they are the easiest item to make. Once mastered, with a little thought these techniques can be applied to most projects. The look of all these belts will be improved if they are slightly raised.

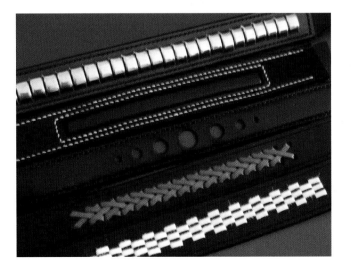

Types of strap work: *(top to bottom)* studded work (clinchers), inlayed work, cut-out work, inlaid plait, weaving.

PRACTICE PROJECT

Studded Dog Collar

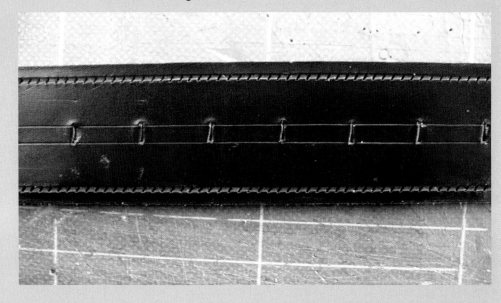

Studded dog collar: centre of strap marked and slits cut for studs.

Use a good quality shoulder with a minimum of 1/8in (3mm) substance. Cut the lengths to suit your own requirements. Other materials required will be a D ring, a buckle of appropriate size and a sufficient number of studs.

Cut and prepare a raised strap as described in Chapter 4. If the leather is of sufficient length, it is permissible to use a single strip folded over to make the strap and lining rather than two separate pieces. It may be felt that the 'raising' of the strap is not necessary. While it gives a better finish, it is not essential and can be left to personal choice.

Mark the strap in the centre, 2in (50mm) in from the end of the buckle return and the last buckle hole. Draw a line down the centre of the strap to join the two marks. This line will act as a guide when centring the clinchers. Set the dividers to the width of the prongs then starting from one end (which end does not matter), walk down the centre line marking the position of the clinchers. If you do not finish exactly on the opposite mark, go one over so that the centre line is covered when the clinchers are placed. There should be ample room on either end to accommodate the extra spacing.

If you are using single ornaments that are to be placed at regular intervals do not use the dividers to mark the centre line, as it will show. Either measure and mark the position of each individual ornament or use a chinagraph pencil in a pair of compasses to mark the centre line. These have high wax content, and the resulting marks can be wiped off.

Use an ordinary wood chisel with 1/8in (3mm) blade to cut the slots for the clinchers. (Chisels with blades this small are difficult to find; therefore, sharpening the end of a narrow bladed screwdriver also works.) Depending on the thickness of the prongs it is occasionally necessary to reset the position of the slots as the clinchers become too tight. Hence, cut the slots in third lots (i.e. if there were 12 slots in total, cut the first 4 and fit the clinchers; then cut the next 4 and so on).

Push the prongs of the clinchers through the slots, then fold them over towards the centre of the clincher, ensuring that they are firmly fixed. When fixing the clinchers it is good practice to turn them onto a scrap piece of leather to protect the finished surface. Do not tap the prongs with a hammer as this could flatten the raised surfaces. When all the clinchers are in place, position the buckle, keeper and D ring, glue and pin the two pieces together and stitch. Finish in the normal manner.

PRACTICE PROJECT

Cut-Out, Inlaid, Inlaid Plait and Woven Belts

CUT-OUT BELT

This type of belt is made in the same manner as a lined strap. Cut the strap, lining and looping and prepare in the normal fashion. Decide on the pattern to be used, mark it onto the strap and cut it out. Edge shaving and dyeing around the grain side of the cut-outs will give a more professional finish. Position the buckle and keeper, glue the two pieces together and stitch. Take care when gluing not to go over the parts that will show through the cut-outs.

INLAID BELT

Cut and prepare the strap, lining and looping. Then cut out the desired pattern on the belt. Cut pieces of leather to match the cut patterns but ⅛in (3mm) smaller; these are the inlays. Glue soft pieces of leather over the inlays, leaving a generous amount around the edges, and position them into the cut-outs; position the buckle and keepers. Glue the pieces together and stitch. Stitch around the inlays if required; a contrasting thread colour may also add to the project. In our example we have interspersed the diamond shapes with domed studs.

INLAID PLAIT

In this technique, lacing is used to form a plait along the surface of the leather. This is only suited to lined items. Two lines of holes are required. Mark two parallel lines ¼in (6mm) apart, equidistant to the centre of the strap. Using the dividers, mark the hole positions, again, ¼in (6mm) apart. It is important that the holes are in 'pairs'; i.e. directly opposite each other. Punch them out using a No.1 hole punch.

1. Cut a length of lacing and thread a thonging needle onto each end. Starting at the first pair of holes, bring the lacing through the leather from the flesh side and equalize the lacing.
2. Go forward to the third pair of holes and pass the needles through from the grain side; then come back through the second pair of holes from the flesh side.
3. Go forward to the fourth pair of holes, through from the grain side, then back to the third pair and through from the flesh side. Continue in this manner, skipping one pair of holes on the grain side, then coming back one pair on the flesh side.

To maintain a regular pattern, it is important to ensure that the lacing is laid down in the same order (i.e. the top row of lacing always crosses over the bottom lacing.

To finish, pass the lacing to the flesh side through the last pair of holes. Cut the lacing leaving 4–5in (101–127mm) trailing. Lay the excess lacing between the two rows on the flesh side. When the lining is stitched into place the lacing will be secured. Adjusting the spacing between the holes and the two rows will alter the resultant laced pattern.

WOVEN LACING

This is a simple matter of cutting vertical slits into the strap and weaving the lacing in and out. With a little ingenuity and using different coloured lacing, many designs can be created. For this technique to work effectively the top layer of leather must be relatively thin – approximately ¹⁄₁₆in (1.5mm).

When starting and finishing the weave, leave a tail of approximately 2in (50mm) at the beginning and end of the lacing. When the lining is stitched into place the lacing will be held securely.

PRACTICE PROJECT

Cut-Out, Inlaid, Inlaid Plait and Woven Belts *continued*

INLAID PLAIT

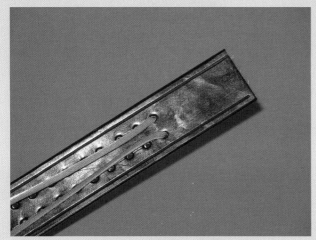

Start on the first pair of holes.

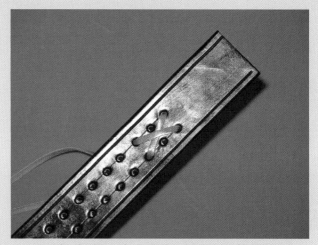

Take the laces through the third pair of holes.

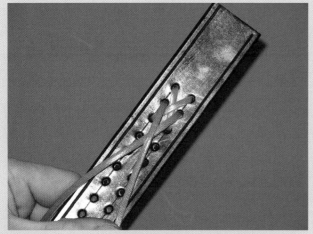

Come back through the second pair of holes and continue the sequence.

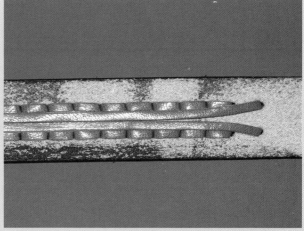

To finish, lay the laces between the stitches; they will be held in place when the lining is stitched into place.

Leather dice cup.

CHAPTER 7

PROJECTS

Simple Projects

These projects only involve the use of scissors, glue, a hole punch and lacing. For all the projects in this section you will require soft leather and PVA glue. Please note that PVA glues used with leather require at least 24 hours drying time before the item can be used.

Chain Belt

The size of the pieces given in the illustration may be altered to suit your own needs. The length of the belt is increased or decreased by adding or subtracting loops. In our example we have used a ¾in (19mm) buckle with a metal fixed keeper and a decorative metal tip on the strap end.

1. Using the given dimensions, make up cardboard patterns for the loops, strap end and buckle end. Cut out the buckle and strap end, and as many loops as required.

General purpose bag, coin pouch and chain belt.

Chain belt dimensions.

Diameter of all outer circles = 2" (50mm)
Diameter of inner circles = 1" (25mm)

Buckle chape

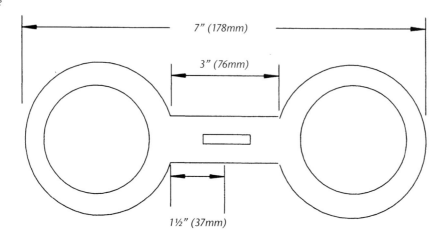

Strap end

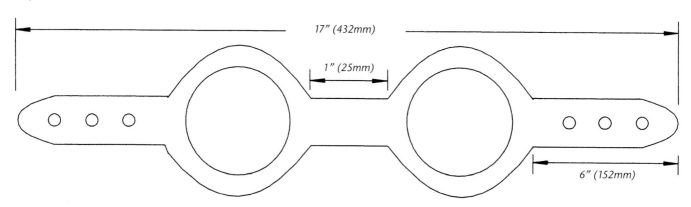

Chain links

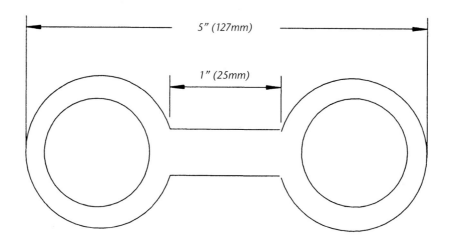

2. If a leather fixed keeper is to be used, cut a strip of leather and make it up as a running keeper. Position the buckle and keeper, and glue the piece, ensuring that the leather before and after the keeper is stuck fast.

3. Working from the buckle end, add and glue as many loops as required to make up the desired length. To allow the loops to move, only glue the circular parts, not the ends.

4. Finally, glue the strap end into place and punch the holes.

CHAIN BELT

RIGHT: Placing leather and metal keepers.

BELOW: Adding loops.

Coin Pouch

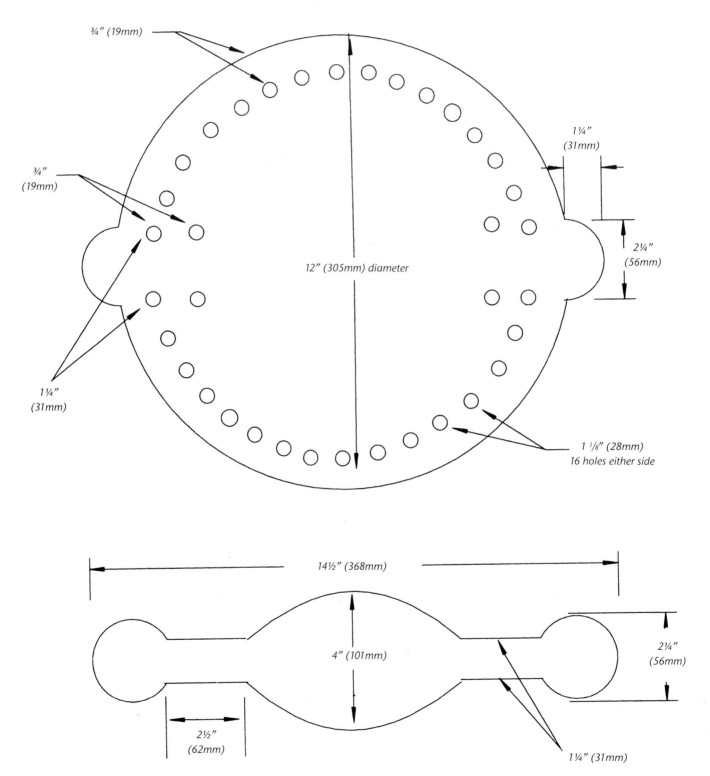

Coin pouch dimensions.

¾" (19mm)

¾"
(19mm)

1¼"
(31mm)

12" (305mm) diameter

1¼"
(31mm)

2¼"
(56mm)

1 ⅛" (28mm)
16 holes either side

14½" (368mm)

4" (101mm)

2¼"
(56mm)

2½"
(62mm)

1¼" (31mm)

Two lengths of lacing, cord or a shoelace, will be required to form the closure around the top of the pouch. Depending on the thickness of the laces used the size of the punched holes and the spacing between them may need adjusting. Here we have used a $5/64$ in (2mm) round leather lace.

1. Make cardboard patterns from the given dimensions. Then mark and cut the leather.
2. Position and glue the centre piece; this slightly stiffens the centre which helps to maintain the shape. Carefully punch out the holes using a No. 6 hole punch.
3. Take one of the laces. Starting from the inside on the lower set of holes, bring the lace to the front and equalize the two halves. Cross the laces and thread them through the holes directly above. Continue threading the lace in and out of the holes on either side of the circle until they meet at the opposite end. Using the remaining lace, repeat the process from the opposite side. Grasp the laces on either side of the pouch and pull. This should bring the leather together and form the shape. Trim the laces to the desired length, not forgetting to leave enough length to allow the pouch to open.
4. Cut two discs of leather, one approximately 1 in (25mm) in diameter and the other ¾in (19mm), and glue them together (using contrasting colours will give a better effect). Punch a No. 6 hole in the centre and thread it over the end of one of the laces. Knot the ends of the lace to secure. Repeat the process on the remaining lace. These discs are pushed close to the pouch when closed and help to stop it from springing open.

COIN POUCH

TOP:
Patterns and cut pieces.

MIDDLE:
To start each side, bring the lace through the bottom pair of holes.

BOTTOM:
Cross the laces and thread them through the outside holes around the circumference to the opposite side.

Slip the disc over the laces and knot the ends to secure.

General Purpose Bag

This bag can be used for carrying moderately heavy items, but not strong enough for loads of tins and jars. If a stronger construction is required, stitch the gussets and handles using a saddle stitch.

1. As this item is made up of rectangular pieces there is no real need to make patterns. Mark and cut all the required pieces to size, and punch the holes using a No. 1 hole punch. If a thinner cord is used to fill the handle the widths of the handle strips will require adjusting.

2. Make up the centre of the handles first. Take the strips of leather cut for the handles and lay them flat on the worktop. Glue the filler cord in the centre, 2½in (62mm) from either end. Fold the leather over the cord, and lace along the length of the cord using a running stitch. Leave a 'tail' of approximately 20in (508mm) at the beginning and end of the lacing.

3. Open the ends of the handle and glue them to the main body of the bag. Position the ends of the handle 3in (76mm) from the top of the bag and 2½in (62mm) in from the edge.

4. Punch through the main body of the bag following the line of holes on the end of the handle (this ensures that they are lined up exactly). Using the lace left on the ends of the handle, attach the handle to the bag. To finish the lacing, place a knot as close to the work as possible on the inside of the bag. Repeat the process with the remaining handle.

5. Line up the first hole on the gusset with the corresponding hole on the bag and attach the gussets using a whip stitch.

General purpose bag dimensions.

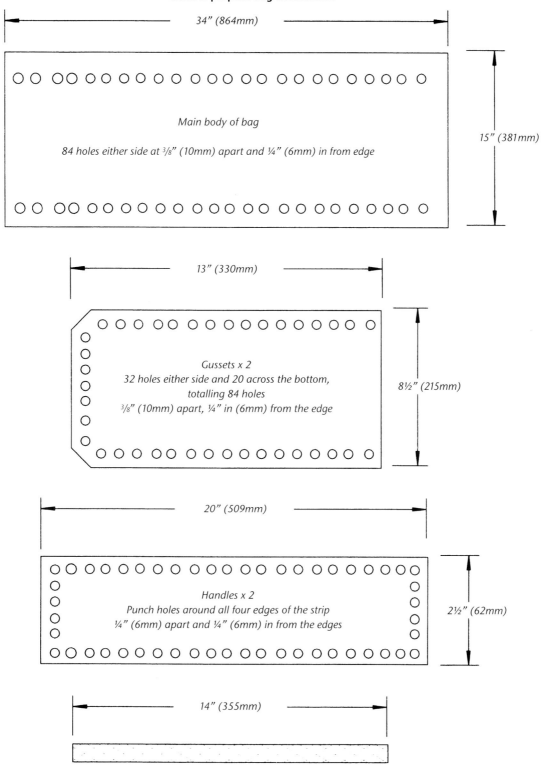

34" (864mm)

Main body of bag

84 holes either side at ⅜" (10mm) apart and ¼" (6mm) in from edge

15" (381mm)

13" (330mm)

Gussets x 2
32 holes either side and 20 across the bottom,
totalling 84 holes
⅜" (10mm) apart, ¼" in (6mm) from the edge

8½" (215mm)

20" (509mm)

Handles x 2
Punch holes around all four edges of the strip
¼" (6mm) apart and ¼" (6mm) in from the edges

2½" (62mm)

14" (355mm)

Filler cord ⁹⁄₁₆" (14mm) diameter

GENERAL PURPOSE BAG

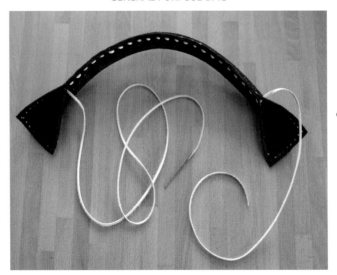

LEFT:
Rolled handle completed; the laces are left long so that they can be used to stitch the handle to the bag.

BELOW LEFT:
Handle glued into position.

ABOVE RIGHT:
Punching the holes once the handles are in position ensures that they are in line.

RIGHT:
Stitching the gussets using a whip stitch.

Leather dice cup and storage box.

Stitched Projects

Small Storage Box

Although we have used a red vegetable tanned shoulder, the box can be decorated by stamping or carving if natural vegetable tanned leather is used. As we are using a large stitch mark, use 18/5 or 18/6 thread.

1. Cut the pieces to the dimensions given. (The lid is slightly larger than the bottom piece of the box to allow for an easier fit.)
2. Using the skiver or splitting machine, reduce the thickness of the insert (Part C) by approximately half.
3. Using a No. 2 edge shave, edge shave the grain surfaces only as follows:
   - Parts C and E (top edge only)
   - Part D (top and bottom edges)
4. On parts A, B, D and E, place a groove line $^3/_{16}$ in (4.5mm) in from the edge around all sides. If required, edge dye all pieces. Then stitch mark the areas shown using a 4 per inch (25mm) stitch marker. It is important that the stitch marks on the ends of parts D and E line up exactly when the pieces are folded together.
5. Stitch the insert (C) to the top edge of the side piece (D). The insert should be positioned so that half of its width and the shaved edge is visible. As the insert (C) is ¼in (6mm) shorter than the side piece (D), there will be $^1/_8$ in (3mm) gap on either side.
6. Fold the two ends of Part D together and place them into the stitching clams. Using a cross stitch (as shown in the illustration), stitch the ends together.
7. Insert the disc that forms the base of the box (A) and stitch into place. Using a saddle stitch and working from the side piece (D), angle the awl so that it emerges in the groove line. As the disc is not stitched marked, care must be taken to get the stitches evenly spaced.
8. Stitch the bottom edge of E with a saddle stitch. This line of stitching is for decoration purposes only. Repeat points 6 and 7 to construct the lid.

Round box dimensions.

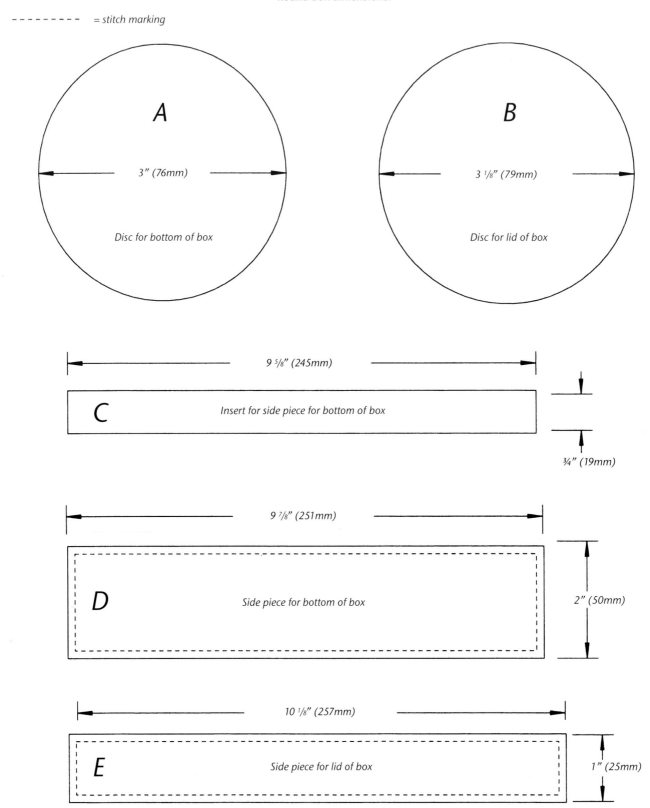

- - - - - - - - - = stitch marking

A

3" (76mm)

Disc for bottom of box

B

3 1/8" (79mm)

Disc for lid of box

9 5/8" (245mm)

C

Insert for side piece for bottom of box

3/4" (19mm)

9 7/8" (251mm)

D

Side piece for bottom of box

2" (50mm)

10 1/8" (257mm)

E

Side piece for lid of box

1" (25mm)

STORAGE BOX

RIGHT:
Insert stitched into place.

BELOW LEFT:
Front view of cross stitch.

ABOVE RIGHT:
Back view of cross stitch.

RIGHT:
Stitching the lid into place (angle the awl so that the stitches come out in the groove line).

Instructions for the cross stitch.

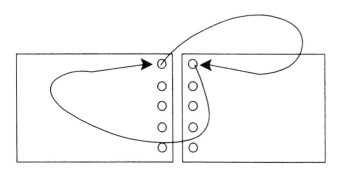

Step 1: Bring the needles through from the back of the work to the front. Push them through the adjacent stitch hole to the back of the work.

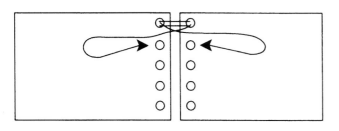

Step 2: On the back of the work, push the needles through the adjacent stitch hole and bring the needles to the front. This forms a double stitch. Push the needles through the stitch holes immediately below and adjacent from the front of the work to the back.

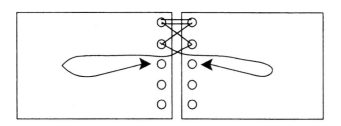

Step 3: On the back of the work, push the needles through the adjacent stitch hole back to the front of the work. Pull the stitch tight and repeat the process.

Dice Cup

This dice cup is assembled in the same manner as the round storage box, with the exception that the two ends will be stitched together with a butt stitch. This is the same as a saddle stitch except that the stitches come out in the middle of the leather. For this reason it is best preformed with heavier leathers. Here we have used a $^{13}/_{64}-{}^{7}/_{32}$in (5–5.50mm) leather. The ends may be joined using the cross stitch.

1. Cut and prepare the pieces in accordance with the illustration. Stitch mark using a 4 per inch (25mm) stitch marker. As with the box it is important that the stitch marks on the ends line up exactly when the piece is folded. Use 18/5 or 18/6 thread for stitching.

2. Glue a piece of felt or suede onto the flesh side of the base and side piece. Along the top of the side piece, fold the suede/felt back on itself to form a seam and stitch it into place. Trim the suede/felt on the bottom edge by an

amount equal to the thickness of the base. This allows the base to be inserted without disturbing the lining.

3. The butt stitch is easier to perform if the stitch marks are pre-pricked. Angle the awl so that it comes out in the centre of the leather. Fold the ends together and following the line of holes, stitch together in the same manner as a saddle stitch. As the leather needs to be manipulated

to locate the holes, it is easier to hold the work in your hands rather than in the stitching clams. When pulling the stitches tight, ensure the thread is pulled in line with the stitches. Pulling in an upward direction could cause the stitch to rip through the leather.

4. Insert the base and stitch together using the same technique used when making the round box.

Dice cup.

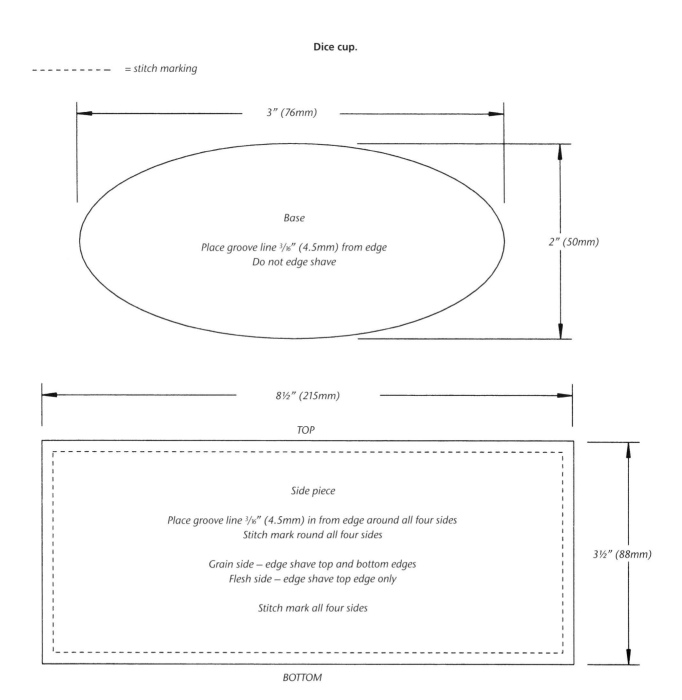

- - - - - - - - - = stitch marking

3" (76mm)

2" (50mm)

Base

Place groove line ³/₁₆" (4.5mm) from edge
Do not edge shave

8½" (215mm)

TOP

Side piece

Place groove line ³/₁₆" (4.5mm) in from edge around all four sides
Stitch mark round all four sides

Grain side – edge shave top and bottom edges
Flesh side – edge shave top edge only

Stitch mark all four sides

3½" (88mm)

BOTTOM

DICE CUP

LEFT:
Lining turned in and stitched to form a seam along the top.

BELOW LEFT:
Pricking out stitch holes (angle the awl so that it comes out in the centre of the leather).

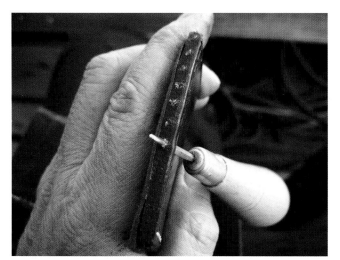

ABOVE RIGHT:
Pulling the two ends together using the butt stitch.

LEFT:
The completed seam.

Equestrian Projects

The two items described in this section are made in a variety of sizes and in the case of bridles, styles. It is beyond the scope of this book to give every size and style, but the construction techniques are similar throughout the ranges.

Stirrup Leathers

These stirrup leathers are made from a top grade vegetable tanned stirrup butt, $^{13}/_{64}-\,^{7}/_{32}$ in (5–5.5mm) using 18/5 or 18/6 threads for stitching. You will also require two 1in (25mm) stirrup buckles (stainless steel buckles are best).

Stirrup leathers are always made as a pair. They are one of the few items of tack (horse equipment) where the flesh side is treated as the grain side (i.e. all work is performed on the flesh side). This is because the flesh side will stretch at the point where the leathers go through the stirrup iron, whereas the grain side would eventually crack. It is important that both leathers are identical – otherwise the rider will be sitting lopsided.

PREPARATION

Cut two strips of leather, 1in (25mm) wide by 60in (1524mm) long. Shape the thickest ends into egg points, and check that both strips are of equal lengths. Stirrup leather buckles have a bar below the buckle tongue. The buckle return is wrapped around this bar dispensing with the need for a crew hole. Edge shave, skive and punch out the holes in accordance with the illustration. Use a No. 3 or No. 4 edge shave and a No. 22 oval hole punch (or a No. 6 round punch if oval punch is unavailable). Finally edge dye the two straps. As we are working on the flesh side it is not necessary to crease the straps.

STITCH MARKING

For safety reasons, stirrup leathers should always have three rows of stitching; each row should be a minimum of 1½in (37mm) in length. The buckle returns must be stitched together with one continuous length of thread.

Once placed into the stitching clams, stitch marks on the flesh side of the leather are sometimes difficult to see. To ensure that the stitch marks are visible, strike the stitch marker with a heavier blow than usual.

CAUTIONARY NOTE

There are safety aspects to take into consideration when making equestrian products. If these items are to be used on a horse, the materials specified (i.e. type of leather, thread and furnishings) must not be substituted. Only use leather that has been specifically tanned for the equestrian trade. The instructions given must be adhered to, and if you are in any doubt about the finished product do not put it on a horse.

Referring to the illustration, use a 7 per inch (25mm) stitch marker and mark the two outside rows first, ⅛in (3mm) in from the edge. The centre line of stitch marks should start one stitch below the two outside rows.

CONSTRUCTION

Fold the buckle return so that the end is in line with the last stitch marks on the outside rows. Dampen the end and tap it with a hammer (refer to Chapter 4 for techniques on folding returns). Using a saddle stitch and 18/5 or 18/6 thread, stitch the two outside rows first. At the end of the second row, take both threads to the back of the work and twist them together. Cross to the centre row and continue stitching. The stitching on stirrup leathers comes under a lot of wear, so ensure that the stitches are hammered flat when complete.

The holes on stirrup leathers are normally numbered so that they can be levelled at a glance. As many still consider the number 13 unlucky, we always use an even number of holes, either 12 or 14. Place the numbers below the hole using a numbering stamp.

Cavason Bridle

The leather used for this bridle must be a top quality vegetable tanned bridle butt of 3.5–4mm substance. With bridles the comfort of the horse is of paramount importance. Therefore, the buckle returns are reversed (turned grain to grain and punched from the flesh side) and the best stitching is on the side nearest the horse. The sizes given for this bridle are for a 14.2 hand cob.

Stirrup leather dimensions.

- - - - - - - = *stitch marking*

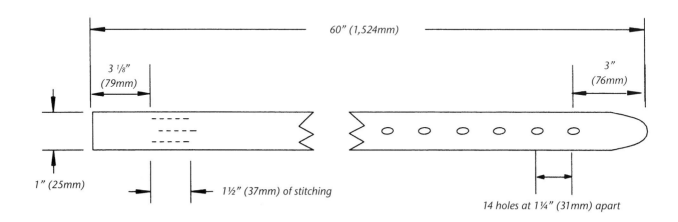

Edge shaving and skiving areas.

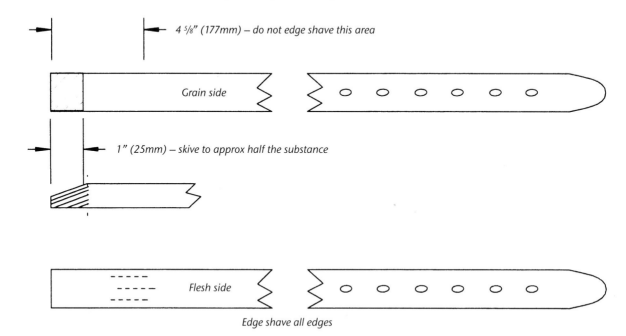

STIRRUP LEATHERS

Cavason bridle and stirrup leathers.

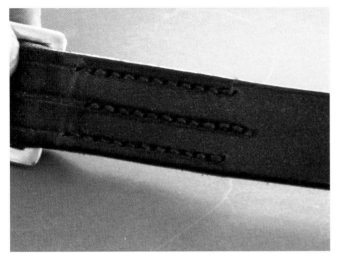

Stitch marking on stirrup leathers.

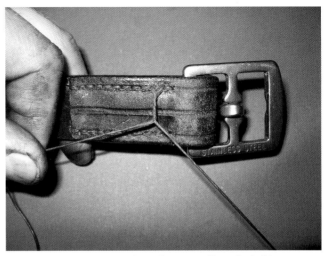

Crossing the threads to the centre line of stitching.

Materials

Cut strips of leather to the following lengths:

Pieces	Measurements
1 x Headpiece	44in (1118mm) × 1⅛in (28mm)
1 x Browband	19¾in (502mm) × ⅝in (16mm)
2 x Cheek pieces	10½in (267mm) × ⅝in (16mm)
1 x Noseband	28in (711mm) × 1⅛in (28mm)
1 x Noseband head strap	½in (12mm) × 32in (813mm)
1 x Noseband cheek	½in (12mm) × 9½in (241mm)
1 x Looping	⁵⁄₁₆in (8mm) × 15in (381mm) approximately
2 x Billet platforms	⅝in (16mm) × 2⅜in (60mm)
1 x Noseband buckle chapes	3in (76mm) × ⅝in (16mm)

The billet platforms and noseband buckle chape (leather to secure a furnishing) need to be reduced to half their substance. It is easier to cut a ⅝in strip of leather approximately 8in (203mm) long, reduce the substance of the entire strip and then cut the pieces. To complete the bridle you will also require:

■ 3 x ⅝in (16mm) bridle buckles
■ 2 x ½in (12mm) bridle buckles
■ 2 x hook studs

Assembly

In reality the processes of cutting, preparing, edge dyeing, creasing and stitch marking would all be done together. For ease of description the complete processes for each individual piece have been described. All buckle returns are 1½in (37mm) in from the end with 1in (25mm) of stitching behind the crew hole. Stitch marking is done using an 8 per inch (25mm) stitch marker. A saddle stitch is used throughout, except when making up running keepers where a back stitch is used. (*See* Chapter 4 for methods of making up buckle returns and keepers.)

HEADPIECE

The throat lash should buckle on the near side of the horse (left side when viewing from the back), but unfortunately it is very easy to make it the wrong way round. If the headpiece is cut as shown in the illustration it will be correct.

1. Referring to the illustration, set the dividers to ½in (12mm). Working along the top edge, draw a line extending 7½in (190mm) from A to B.
2. Measure 12in (305mm) from B to C. Again working along the top edge, draw a line to connect D and C.
3. Punch a hole at points B and C with a No. 1 hole punch. The hole helps to prevent the leather from ripping when in use. Working away from the holes towards the ends, carefully cut down the lines B to A and C to D.
4. Measure 7½in (190mm) from C to E and cut the lower strap at point E. If done correctly the resultant piece should look like the illustration, with a ½in (12mm) throat lash on the top and ⅝in (16mm) cheek straps below.
5. Remembering that the buckle returns are reversed, punch the crew hole on the flesh side of the throat lash. Cut the bridle points as shown, and punch the holes. Skive the ends of the bridle points to approximately half their substance, and prepare the buckle return. Edge shave all

Bridle point dimensions to be used with cavason bridle.

Cut all the bridle points on the bridle to these dimensions:

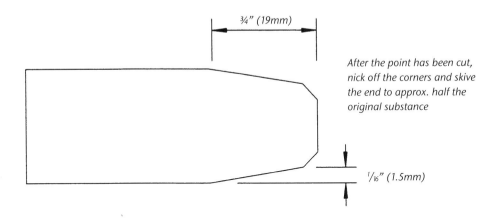

¾" (19mm)

After the point has been cut, nick off the corners and skive the end to approx. half the original substance

$^1/_{16}$" (1.5mm)

Cavason bridle: headpiece.

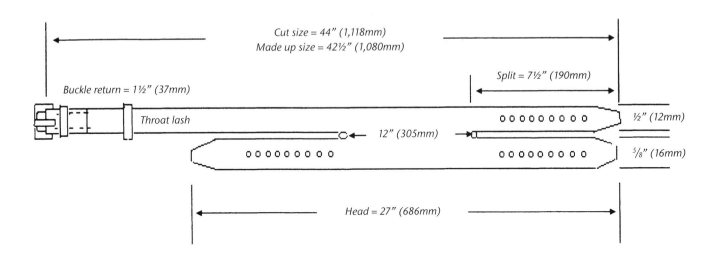

Cut size = 44" (1,118mm)
Made up size = 42½" (1,080mm)

Split = 7½" (190mm)

Buckle return = 1½" (37mm)

Throat lash

½" (12mm)

12" (305mm)

$^5/_8$" (16mm)

Head = 27" (686mm)

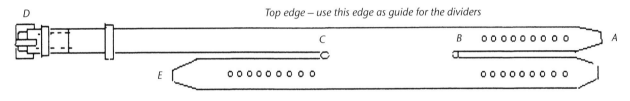

Top edge – use this edge as guide for the dividers

D

C

B

A

E

Punch 9 holes at $^5/_8$" (16mm) apart, starting 1½" (37mm) from the ends edges (not the join of the buckle return) using a No. 2 edge shave.

6. Edge dye and then using a screw crease set to approximately $\frac{1}{16}$in (1.5mm) crease around all the edges on the grain side. At the top of the splits, use a single crease to join the crease lines. On the flesh side of the throat lash, stitch mark the buckle return.

7. Make a running keeper to fit the throat lash and block it up. Fit it over the throat lash, then stitch the buckle into place with a fixed keeper.

BROWBAND

Prepare the browband as shown in the illustration. To prevent the browband from rubbing, the ends must be skived very thin. To assemble the browband, fold the end so that the edge is in line with the last stitch mark. Place the work into the stitching clams, ensuring that it does not move out of position, and stitch together.

CHEEK PIECES

Each cheek piece will require three fixed keepers (one behind the buckle and two on the billet platform), a running keeper and a billet platform. Cut and prepare the pieces in accordance with the illustration. Skive the bridle point to half its original substance and edge shave. The hole on the end of the cheek piece is punched with a keyhole punch. If this is not available follow the instructions shown. Edge shave, dye and crease. Stitch mark the buckle return and the position where the billet platforms will be placed.

Make and block up the running keepers. Stitch the buckles into place, and slip the running keepers over the strap. Next the billet platforms are stitched in place. Place the first stitch over the end of the platform, then complete another stitch. Position the first keeper and continue stitching. The second keeper is positioned two complete stitches in from the opposite end of the platform. (Beginners may find it easier to pin the platforms into position before beginning the stitching.) Cross over and stitch the other side in the same manner as a buckle return.

NOSEBAND

This is another piece that is frequently stitched wrongly. Ensure that the pieces are assembled as shown in the illustration. Cut and prepare the pieces in accordance with the instructions.

1. To shape the noseband lay the strip with the grain side upmost. Measure 5in (127mm) from A to B, then 1in (25mm) from B to C, marking each measurement on either side of the strip. Set the dividers to ¼in (6mm) and draw a line on both sides from B to A. Join points C to B using a ruler. Carefully cut either side, then make the bridle point. At D cut the corners at 45 degrees.

2. Make up the cheek with a running and fixed keeper.

3. Position the buckle chape so that the end lines up with the end of the noseband. (Pin the chape into place if desired.) Stitch up to the buckle, then skip over one stitch mark to make a large stitch over the buckle bar. Go back over the bar and then come forward and continue stitching. (There should be three strands of thread over the buckle bar). When the same point is reached on the opposite side, repeat the process, then continue to the end of the stitch run.

4. Position the cheek approximately ¼in (6mm) from C and stitch into position. The head strap is then positioned and stitched into place 12in (305mm) from the cheek.

Finishing

Block up all fixed keepers, and dye and polish all joins. Recrease any stitching where the best stitching is on the grain side. Finally feed and polish the bridle.

Cavason bridle: browband.

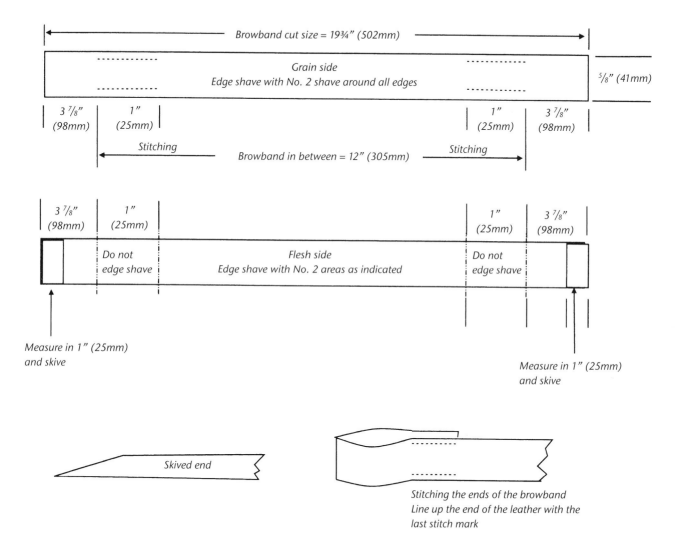

Browband cut size = 19¾" (502mm)

Grain side
Edge shave with No. 2 shave around all edges

⁵⁄₈" (41mm)

3 ⁷⁄₈"
(98mm)

1"
(25mm)

1"
(25mm)

3 ⁷⁄₈"
(98mm)

Stitching

Browband in between = 12" (305mm)

Stitching

3 ⁷⁄₈"
(98mm)

1"
(25mm)

1"
(25mm)

3 ⁷⁄₈"
(98mm)

Do not
edge shave

Flesh side
Edge shave with No. 2 areas as indicated

Do not
edge shave

Measure in 1" (25mm)
and skive

Measure in 1" (25mm)
and skive

Skived end

Stitching the ends of the browband
Line up the end of the leather with the
last stitch mark

Cavason bridle: cheek pieces.

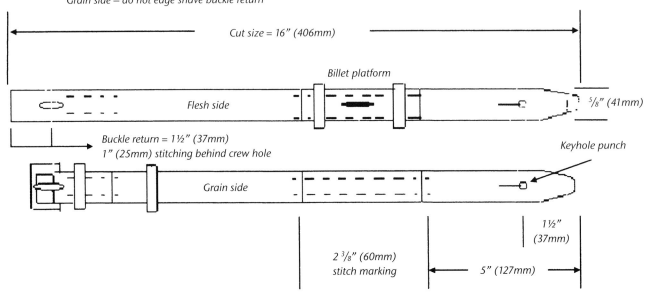

Use No. 2 edge shave
Flesh side – do not edge shave where billet platform sits
Grain side – do not edge shave buckle return

Cut size = 16" (406mm)

Billet platform

Flesh side

⁵/₈" (41mm)

Buckle return = 1½" (37mm)
1" (25mm) stitching behind crew hole

Keyhole punch

Grain side

1½"
(37mm)

2 ³/₈" (60mm)
stitch marking

5" (127mm)

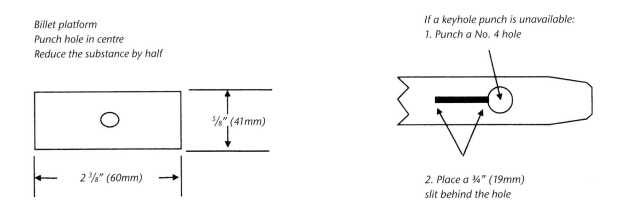

Billet platform
Punch hole in centre
Reduce the substance by half

⁵/₈" (41mm)

2 ³/₈" (60mm)

If a keyhole punch is unavailable:
1. Punch a No. 4 hole

2. Place a ¾" (19mm)
slit behind the hole

Cavason bridle: noseband.

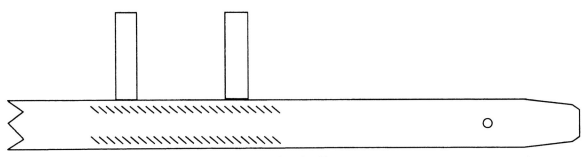

Positioning of billet platform fixed keepers.

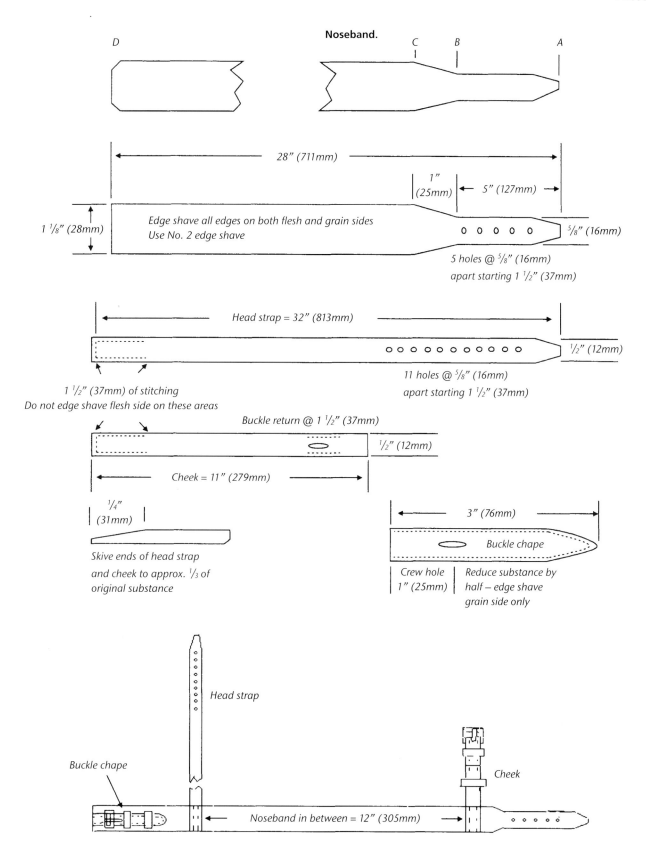

Noseband.

D   C   B   A

28" (711mm)

1"
(25mm)   5" (127mm)

1 ¹/₈" (28mm)

Edge shave all edges on both flesh and grain sides
Use No. 2 edge shave

O O O O O   ⁵/₈" (16mm)

5 holes @ ⁵/₈" (16mm)
apart starting 1 ¹/₂" (37mm)

Head strap = 32" (813mm)

o o o o o o o o o o o   ¹/₂" (12mm)

11 holes @ ⁵/₈" (16mm)
apart starting 1 ¹/₂" (37mm)

1 ¹/₂" (37mm) of stitching
Do not edge shave flesh side on these areas

Buckle return @ 1 ¹/₂" (37mm)

¹/₂" (12mm)

Cheek = 11" (279mm)

¹/₄"
(31mm)

Skive ends of head strap
and cheek to approx. ¹/₃ of
original substance

3" (76mm)

Buckle chape

Crew hole
1" (25mm)   Reduce substance by
half – edge shave
grain side only

Head strap

Buckle chape

Cheek

Noseband in between = 12" (305mm)

155

CAVASON BRIDLE

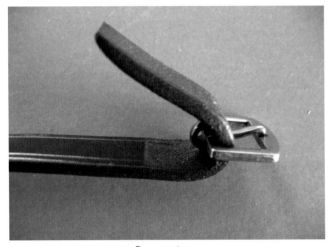

Reverse turn.

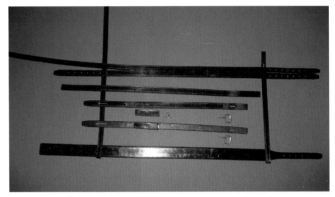

Parts of the bridle cut and prepared ready for stitching.

Using the single crease around the top of the splits on the headpiece.

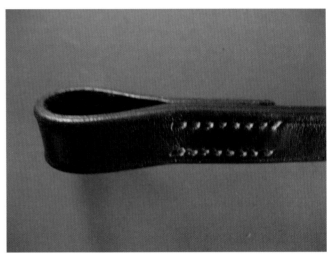

Completed end of the browband.

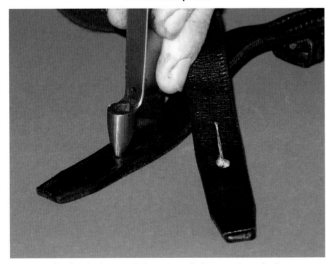

The keyhole punch in use and the resultant hole.

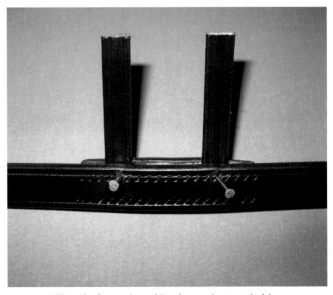

Billet platform pinned in place prior to stitching.

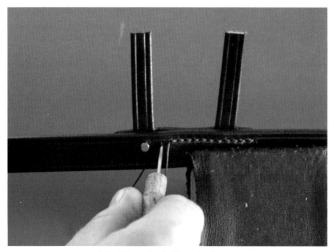

Stitching the billet platform.

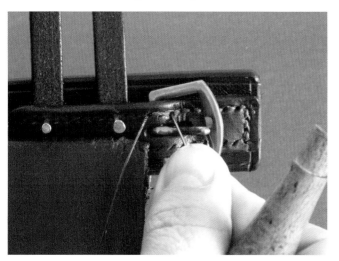

Stitching over the buckle.

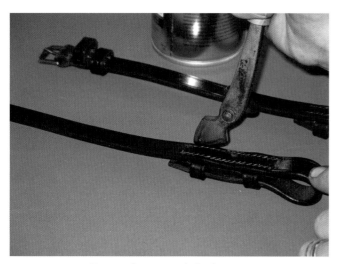

Re-creasing over stitched areas.

Noseband buckle chape pinned into position.

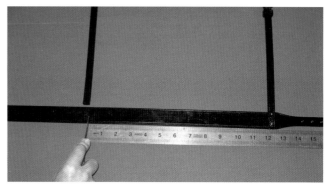

Positioning the noseband head strap.

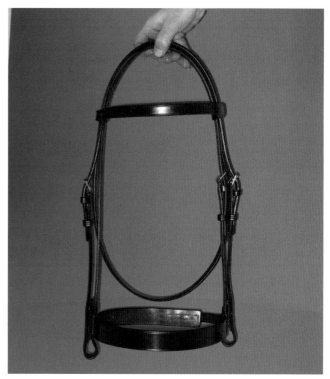

The completed bridle.

A hole starting to stretch and weaken on a beloved belt.

CHAPTER 8

CARE AND REPAIR

Care

As already discussed, leather was once a living, breathing skin, maintained by the natural oils produced by the animal. Once tanned, in order to keep the leather in good condition, the natural oils need to be maintained artificially. Caring for leather is generally a case of cleaning, feeding (often called conditioning) and protecting it. Depending on the type and use it may also require the occasional polish.

There are many differing opinions on how to care for leather. Each person will have their own favourite methods. The guidelines given here are based on techniques used in our workshop and advice given from professional bodies, and it is not the intention to disparage anyone else's methods.

General Care

Leather should be kept away from excessive heat as this can dry out the oils, causing the fibre structure to become brittle and the grain to crack. Prolonged exposure to direct sunlight can have the same effect and, in addition, cause the dye to fade. Wet leather should be allowed to dry naturally away from direct heat sources. Wet items such as shoes and boots should be stuffed with old newspapers so that they maintain their shape as they dry. Any dirt should be wiped off immediately using a cloth and clean water. (Muddy boots can be brushed off when dry.) Do not use any chemicals such as spot cleaners and detergents that are not specifically designed for leather.

Never store leather in plastic as this encourages the growth of mildew and bacteria which will ruin the item. Store in a cool dry place, away from direct sunlight and heat. If it is necessary to store it in a bag, ensure that it is made of a breathable material.

Cleaners, Feeds, Protectors and Polishes

A quick search will reveal the vast array of leather cleaners, feeds and polishes, many claiming to be multipurpose. Read the instructions carefully and avoid anything that contains petroleum or mineral oils as these can damage the leather over a period of time. Also avoid any that leave a tacky residue on the surface as this will attract dirt. If possible, always seek advice from the manufacturer as to which products to use on specific items.

Exercise extreme care when using cleaners, protectors or polishes on any item that you have made, especially if it has a painted surface. Some products may strip off any finish or dye already applied, and many tend to react with leather paints.

It is extremely important to recognize the type of leather you are dealing with as the differing finishes will require different techniques. Before applying any of these products, always test them for colour distortion and dye fastness on a small area that will not be seen. Always read the instructions, and work in a well ventilated area, as some of these items are fairly powerful and can cause irritations.

CLEANING

The use of leather cleaners is very subjective. On pigmented and semi-aniline leathers (*see* Chapter 2) there is a danger of stripping off the protective coating, and on aniline leathers they could cause greater damage. If in doubt do not use them, and seek the advice of a professional cleaner. General cleaning can be carried out by following the instructions below.

Pigmented and semi-aniline leathers should be cleaned with warm water with a little pure soap dissolved into it. Wet a cloth with the soapy water (micro fibre cloths work well) and wring it out thoroughly so the cloth is only damp. Wipe over the surface using circular motions. Then repeat the process using clean water. It is important not to soak the leather surface. Aniline leathers (here we are including any leather without a protective coating) should be cleaned in the same manner using only warm water. However, stains on these types of leather can be difficult, if not impossible, to remove. Do not rub too hard. Any spillages should be cleaned up immediately, soaking them up with a paper towel or cloth. Dab the area, as wiping may spread the spillage causing damage over a wider area.

There seems to be a common misconception that saddle soap is the thing to use for cleaning leather; this probably comes from the name. Anyone who has ever worked with saddle soap can tell you it is messy, it can stain certain leathers, often streaks, does not clean well and leaves the surface with a tacky residue. While it does soften leather if used correctly, there are much better cleaners on the market.

FEEDING
Leather feeds contain combinations of oils, wax, lanoline or fats. Apply the feed in accordance with the instructions or with a soft cloth working across the surface in small circles (this generates friction, which helps the feed penetrate into the leather fibres). Time should then be allowed for the feed to soak into the leather before buffing it off.

Leather Oils
The belief that Neatsfoot oil rots stitching has been around for a few years. This is untrue – it is not the oils that rot the stitching but the moisture content trapped in the leather by the over application of oils. Leather oils (Neatsfoot included) are great for softening leather quickly and restoring the suppleness of old dry leather. The major problem with these products is that people tend to use too much. Oils soak into the leather and act on the fibre structure. Too much oil causes the fibres to swell, which in turn softens the leather making it more prone to stretching. Leather absorbs moisture from its surroundings. Too much oil will stop the leather breathing, which prevents the moisture from escaping. Over time, this could rot the leather and the stitching.

In the tanneries, oils are applied while the leather is damp, which helps the oil penetrate the fibres. If applied to dry leather it is like painting a freshly plastered wall – the surface sucks the paint in like blotting paper. Dampen the item, then apply the oil, leave for twenty-four hours, then wipe off any excess. Remember, a little at a time is best.

PROTECTION
There are specific products on the market which will prevent moisture from being absorbed by the leather. On certain items, such as leather upholstered furniture, their use may be necessary to prevent spillages from soaking into the surface before it can be cleaned up. It is extremely important to get the product that matches the type of leather, so always seek professional advice.

POLISHING
Whether to polish an item is down to personal choice; my personal view is that leather looks better if allowed to age naturally. The problem with polishes is that some can be quite abrasive, and they can also clog the fibre structure and dry out the leather. Some will also contain a colouring agent which can be transferred onto other items.

SUEDE AND NUBUCK
There are many cleaners and restorers available for these types of leather. They normally come in an aerosol form and may also involve the use of a suede brush. Apply them in accordance with the instructions.

Repairs

Having worked through this book you should have acquired enough knowledge to carry out simple repairs. Armed with the knowledge and techniques of how items are constructed, it should not be too difficult to work out how to repair them. However, there are a few repairs which may have you wondering how to go about it.

BELT HOLE REPAIR

Repairing the hole by placing a strip over all the holes and making a feature of the repair.

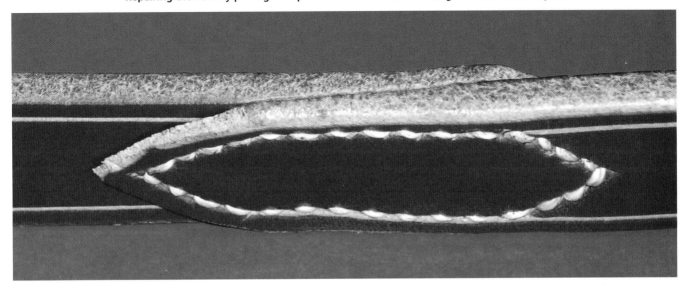

Splicing two pieces of leather together.

Always consider the use of the item, any stress that will be placed on the repair and whether it is easier or safer to re-make the part. In the equestrian trade the splicing of items such as girth straps on saddles and stirrup leathers is never done – these are always replaced.

Re-stitching

This is one of the most common repairs. Often it occurs at points that are under strain, such as bag handles or where the stitching has been rubbing. This is a simple case of using an appropriate type of stitch and following the existing holes, starting and ending two or three stitches over the good stitching. To avoid cutting the good stitches, use a round awl or the needle to open the holes. Before starting, always remove any old stitching as stitching over it looks a mess.

Rips

Rips in leather furniture or clothing are extremely difficult to repair neatly and should be left to a professional. However, if you are intent on trying it yourself there are various methods that can be used.

1. Pull and stitch the edges together. Think carefully before using this method. If the repair comes under strain it could tear apart leaving the area looking worse then before.
2. Place a thin piece of leather behind the tear and stick or stitch the edges of the tear to it.
3. Patch a piece of leather over the tear. This is the most effective method but the patch will always be seen, which may be a problem. A method of making patches look more acceptable is to make a feature of the patch, cutting the patch in the shape of an insignia or carving an insignia onto natural vegetable tanned leather so that it looks like it was always meant to be there. Obviously the position of the rip will dictate if this is acceptable. This method can be successfully employed on belts where the holes have stretched or ripped. In our example a contrasting coloured piece of leather was split to approximately half its substance, stitched in place and re-punched.

Splicing

The secret of good splicing is to make it appear as part of the item. To achieve this, square off the broken ends (shaping them into egg points will give a better finish), skive the flesh side on one end and the grain side on the other so that a continuous thickness is maintained when the join is made, overlap the two pieces and stitch together. The amount of overlap will depend on the strain that will be placed on the join; the longer the overlap the stronger it will be. Splicing a piece of leather over the top and bottom of the break is another method that can be employed.

SPLICING BUCKLE RETURNS

This is another fairly common repair and is often caused by poor maintenance. Often people will forget about feeding the areas around the buckles, so the leather dries out and breaks easily. The best method is to remake the buckle return, but this is not always possible as the overall length of the strap will be shortened in the process.

Remove the folded part of the return and all the old stitching. Square off the end and cut a semi-circle in the centre (this allows the buckle tongue to sit right into the strap end when the new piece is joined). Cut a new piece of leather to the same width and double the length of the original return. Reduce the substance to that of the original return and skive the two ends, tapering them down to half of the remaining substance. Place an appropriate size crew punch in the centre of the new piece (halfway between the ends and edges), dye and stitch mark.

Fold the new piece in half, position the buckle and place it over the broken end of the strap; the buckle tongue should fit into the semi-circle. Place the work into the clams and stitch into place using a saddle stitch. The new piece will be covered by the end of the strap once the buckle is fastened.

Shortening Belts

To maintain the overall appearance of the belt they should, if possible, be shortened from the buckle end. If the end is simply 'chopped off', the distance between the buckle hole

BUCKLE CHAPE REPAIR

The buckle has ripped through the end of the chape.

The end of the strap is squared off and skived; a new piece is cut and slipped over the end of the strap.

The completed repair.

and the end of the belt is reduced, which leaves the belt looking unbalanced.

Undo the return and lay the belt flat on the work surface. Measuring from the end of the return (with the return opened out), mark the required distance. Cut the belt at this point and re-make the return exactly as the original. When performed using this method, any allowances for the buckle return are already incorporated.

Bear in mind, the distance the belt is to be reduced by must go past the crew hole so that it can be removed; otherwise there is no alternative but to shorten the belt from the strap end.

Zips

Replacing zips by hand can be an arduous task, with much time and effort spent trying to remove the old one. Having found a matching zip, it is important that it is placed exactly in the same position as the original. Use tack stitches to hold it in place. A neater finish is generally achieved by hand stitching, as the old stitch holes can be followed – a task that is difficult to accomplish with a sewing machine. With most zips the back side will not be visible when secured in place, so it is possible to use a back stitch. This will leave one hand free to manoeuvre the zip so that the spacing between the edge of the leather and the teeth is constant; if this is not done problems closing the zip could occur.

Conclusion

I hope you have enjoyed working through the skills presented in this book, and that you have been inspired to explore the craft of leatherworking further. I cannot emphasize enough, enjoy yourself and you will learn easily and progressively. Approaching any craft without pleasure quickly turns it into a chore, which results in frustration and eventually leads to the craft being dropped.

As you progress through more difficult projects, always take pride in your work and strive to do better. While techniques may be perfected through repetition, repeating a technique over and over soon becomes boring. It is better to practise the techniques by doing simple projects, as provided here. If you feel yourself becoming frustrated, as soon as these feelings arise, put the project down and return to it when you are in a more positive frame of mind.

Leather crafting can bring lasting pleasure and a powerful feeling of accomplishment. You can look forward to the day someone asks, 'Where did you get that?' and you can say, 'I made it!'

LEATHER SUBSTANCES

1mm = 0.39737": 1 iron = 1/48": 1 ounce = 1/64"

Inches	Ounces	Irons	Millimetres
1/64	1	0.75	0.4
1/32	2	1.5	0.8
3/64	3	2.25	1.2
1/16	4	3	1.6
5/64	5	3.75	2
3/32	6	4.5	2.4
7/64	7	5.25	2.8
1/8	8	6	3.2
9/64	9	6.75	3.6
5/32	10	7.5	4
11/64	11	8.25	4.4
3/16	12	9	4.8
13/64	13	9.75	5.2
7/32	14	10.5	5.6
15/64	15	11.25	6
1/4	16	12	6.4
17/64	17	12.75	6.8
9/32	18	13.5	7.2

PUNCH SIZES

Round and Oval

The punch numbers and sizes may vary with different manufacturers.

Round No.	Oval No.	Inches	Millimetres
0	17	5/64"	1.98mm
1	18	3/32"	2.38mm
2	19	7/64"	2.78mm
3	20	1/8"	3mm
4	21	5/32"	4mm
5	22	11/64"	4.36mm
6	23	3/16"	4.76mm
7	24	13/64"	5.16mm
8	25	1/4"	6mm
9	26	9/32"	7.14mm
10	27	5/16"	8mm
11	28	3/8"	10mm
12	29	13/32"	10.32mm
13	30	7/16"	11mm
14	31	1/2"	12mm
15	32	9/16"	14mm
16		5/8"	16mm

Crew (Length of Slot)

Number	Inches	Millimetres
33	1/4"	6mm
34	3/8"	10mm
35	1/2"	12mm
36	5/8"	16mm
37	3/4"	19mm
38	7/8"	22mm
39	1"	25mm
40	1 1/8"	28mm

Edge Shaves

Number	Inches	Millimetres
1	3/64"	1.2mm
2	1/16"	1.5mm
3	5/64"	1.98mm
4	3/32"	2.38mm
5	7/64"	2.78mm
6	1/8"	3mm

GLOSSARY

awl (*stitching*) used to pierce the leather to allow the passage of the needles; (*scratch*) used for marking the leather; (*pointed*) with a round pointed blade, useful when stitching over existing stitching because it does not cut the stitches.

back cut of leather, taken from either side of the spine, that includes the shoulder but not the bellies.

backgrounding making areas within and around a carved design recede into the background by compressing them with a background tool.

back stitch stitch performed with a single needle by coming back one stitch, then forward.

bellies cut of leather from the outer edges of the hide; having a loose fibre structure, they are very stretchy with little tensile strength, and have a spongy feel when compressed, making them unsuitable for most leatherwork projects.

bend another term for *butt* (more commonly used in the shoe trade).

bevelling (1) another term for edge shaving; or (2) when carving, going around the swivel knife cuts with a beveller to bring the design into relief.

burnishing polishing the edge of the leather by rubbing it quickly with a hard surface such as a slicker, bone or burnisher.

butt cut of leather taken from either side of the spine with the bellies and shoulders removed; the best cut of a hide.

butt stitch a stitch used to join two edges together, performed in the same manner as a saddle stitch except the stitches come out in the middle of the leather's thickness.

camouflage texturing certain areas of a carved design.

casing preparing the leather prior to carving.

chape a piece of leather stitched onto another piece of leather to secure a furnishing.

chrome tanned leather tanned using minerals, the most common being chromium salts.

clinchers raised metal studs used to decorate leather.

creasing making an impression on the surface of the leather, normally with a hot creasing tool.

crew hole oblong slot cut into the leather to accommodate the tongues of buckles; normally cut with a crew punch.

currying the finishing process of the tanning procedure; might include splitting to desired thickness, dyeing, fat liquoring, smoothing and stretching, buffing to cover any imperfections and embossing.

cutting patterns usually made from card, giving the exact dimensions and shape of how the leather is to be cut, including any allowances, position of furnishings, etc.

edge shaving removing the leather edges; also known as edging.

egg point the end of a strap cut to an oval shape.

embossing designs that are pressed into the leather by some form of press.

fat liquoring process where the natural fats and oils lost in the tanning process are replaced.

furnishings items such as buckles, rings etc that are attached to the leather.

grooving cutting a line into the surface of the leather.

hide the skin of a large animal.

iron unit of measurement to denote the thickness of leather (more commonly used in the shoe trade).

keeper loop of leather through which the strap passes; (*fixed*) stitched into place; (*running*) left free to slide along the strap.

lacing   (1) a single thin piece of leather used for decorative work; or (2) a decorative method of joining leather.

liming   part of the tanning process where the hides are soaked in lime pits to remove the majority of the hair and fats.

paring   another term for *skiving*.

pickling   part of the tanning process where the hides are progressively moved through pits filled with varying strengths of tanning solution.

race   tool used to cut grooves.

return   part of a leather strap that is folded to accommodate some form of furnishing.

rolling   giving a leather strap a round finish by folding and stitching.

running stitch   simple stitch where the needle is passed in and out down the length of the stitching run.

saddle stitch   stitch performed with a needle on either end of the thread.

saddler's clams   device used to hold the work piece while stitching; made from two pieces of specially shaped wood which are bolted together to form a set of sprung jaws into which the work piece is placed.

scudding   the removal by hand of any hair, flesh or fat left after the liming process.

seeder   tool used to fill in the seed pods of a flower in a carved design.

shading   technique of giving a carved design a three dimensional effect.

shoulder   cut of leather from the top end (head end) of the hide.

side   cut of leather taken from either side of the spine, including the shoulders and bellies.

skin   refers to the skin of smaller animals.

skiving   shaving down the leather to reduce the thickness in places where it would be too bulky, such as on a belt where the leather folds to accommodate the buckle.

slicker   tool used to polish the edges of the leather.

splitting   reducing the substance of the leather by shaving off a layer; often done by machine.

square off   (1) to create a straight edge on a hide by cutting it either down the middle or along the thickest side; or (2) to prepare one end of a strap by cutting it at 90 degrees to the edge.

stamping   (1) impressing a design directly onto the leather surface; or (2) when carving, bringing the design to life with the use of a stamping tool, such as a beveller or shader.

staining   another term for *dyeing*.

stirrup   a loop (normally of leather) serving as a footrest, especially in horseback riding; a stirrup iron is threaded onto the leathers.

stitching pony   device used to hold the work piece while stitching; differs from *saddler's clams* in that the clam part is fixed on one end of a bench.

substance   the thickness of a hide or leather.

Tannery Run   (TR) leather that has left the tannery without sorting or grading.

tannin   chemical substance found in the bark, leaves and seedpods of trees, used for tanning.

tanning   the preservation of skins and hides.

thonging   another term for *lacing*.

transfer pattern   normally a tracing that is transferred onto the surface of the leather to create a carved design.

vegetable tanned   leather tanned using the naturally occurring substance found in the bark, seedpods and leaves of certain trees.

veiner   tool used in carving leather to give the effect of veins on leaves and stems.

working patterns   patterns drawn up in the initial stage giving the made-up size and shape of a project, not including any seam or turning allowances; used to confirm shapes and sizes.

SUPPLIERS

UK Suppliers

Abbey Saddlery & Crafts Ltd
Abbey House
Haig Road, Parkgate Industrial Estate
Knutsford, Cheshire
WA16 8DX
Tel: 01565 650343
Website: www.abbeysaddlery.com

Le Prevo Ltd
No. 1 Charlotte Square
Newcastle upon Tyne
NE1 4XF
Tel: 0191 232 4179
Website: www.leprevo.co.uk

Marcus Gear Ltd
64-66 Hollyhedge Lane
Walsall
West Midlands
WS2 8PZ
Tel: 01922 632 329
Website: www.marcusgear.co.uk

TANDY LEATHER FACTORY
Unit 2 Crofton Oak
North Portway Close
Round Spinney Industrial Estate
Northampton
NN3 8RD
Tel: 01604 647 910
Website: www.tandyleatherfactory.co.uk

US Suppliers

WEAVER LEATHER, LLC
7540 CR 201
PO Box 68
Mt. Hope, Ohio 44660
Tel: Toll Free 800-932-8371
Local & International: 330-674-1782
website: www.weaverleather.com

INDEX